684.1 MOR

Morrison, Amanda.

Simple handmade
 furniture : 23   MANTECA
17X 11/65 ct 7/05
31x 3/14 ct 12/13

D0118832

simple handmade
furniture

23
step-by-step
weekend
projects

simple handmade *furniture*

Amanda Morrison
and
Cally Matthews

LAUREL
GLEN

c o n t

Published in the United States by
Laurel Glen Publishing
An Imprint of the Advantage Publishers Group
5880 Oberlin Drive, San Diego, CA 92121-4794
www.advantagebooksonline.com

Copyright © Cico Books, 2001

Copyright under international, Pan American, and
Universal Copyright Conventions. All rights reserved.
No part of this book may be reproduced or transmitted
in any form or by any means, electronic or mechanical,
including photocopying, recording, or by any
information storage-and-retrieval system, without
written permission from the copyright holder. Brief
passages (not to exceed 1,000 words) may be quoted
for reviews.

All notations of errors or omissions should be
addressed to Laurel Glen Publishing, editorial
department, at the above address. All other
correspondence (author inquiries, permissions and

rights) concerning the content of this book should be
addressed to: Cico Books, 32 Great Sutton Street,
London EC1V ONB.

ISBN 1-57145-330-X

Library of Congress Cataloging-in-Publication Data
Morrison, Amanda.
  Simple handmade furniture: 23 step-by-step weekend
projects / Amanda Morrison and
Cally Matthews.
  p. cm.
  ISBN 1-57145-330-X
  1. Furniture making–Amateurs' manuals. 2.
Woodwork–Amateurs' manuals. I.
  Matthews, Cally. II. Title.

TT195 .M65 2001
684.1–dc21   00-067748

The authors wish to acknowledge Philip Haxell's design
contribution in "The Bathroom."
Photography by Lucinda Symons

Designed by Roger Daniels
Consultancy and project editing by Ian Kearey
Photography managed by Kate Haxell

North American Edition
Publisher: Allen Orso
Managing Editor: JoAnn Padgett
Product Manager: Elizabeth McNulty
Project Editor: Bobby Wong
Assisting Editor: Mana Monzavi

Reproduction by Alliance Graphics, Singapore
Printed in Italy by Editoriale Johnson

1 2 3 4 5 01 02 03 04 05

e n t s

Introduction

If until now your experience with woodworking books has consisted of technical manuals with frightening diagrams and lists of specialized equipment, then think again. *Simple Handmade Furniture* throws away all those preconceptions and instead is a celebration of the versatility of wood.

It doesn't matter if you don't know one end of a jigsaw from the other. This book includes some very simple ideas that are ideal for beginners. They are a perfect way to build confidence, so that after a time, you will feel ready to progress onto more involved pieces.

Like most creative pursuits, once you get the hang of it, woodworking is great fun. It's also very rewarding to be able to step back from a completed project and say "I made that."

What about the cost? If you rush off to your local home improvement store and invest in all the latest equipment, woodworking can become quite expensive. But the good news is that you don't need all the latest gadgets and gizmos; a few key tools are enough to get you started (see "Toolbox" on page 8). When it comes to pricier items like power drills or jigsaws, try borrowing or renting them before you buy. Alternatively, split the cost with a friend who shares your interest. That way you can get a feel for using the equipment without incurring a lot of expense.

In the past, woodworking was seen as a characteristically male interest, but that is no longer true. The equipment available today is much lighter and easier to manage than ever before. If you take a look down the "power tool" aisle of your local home improvement store, you'll notice that manufacturers are developing compact designs with just as much punch as their heavier predecessors. Also, the improved, simplified instructions mean that woodworking appeals to everyone as never before. What are you waiting for?

All you need to get started are a few inspiring ideas—and that's what you will find here. The projects in this book are not only simple to make, but look stylish too. The projects are divided into chapters, each one featuring a different room. The designs vary in complexity but are all quite straightforward. Of course, once you become more confident, you can adapt or modify each project to suit your own style and needs.

Whatever you do, remember to enjoy the challenge and make safety a priority.

Safety

It goes without saying that safety is a key issue. Always follow these basic rules and use your common sense. It is never worth the risk of taking shortcuts where safety is concerned.

● Always wear a mask and goggles when cutting wood or MDF, and work in a well-ventilated room if possible.

● When using power tools, follow the manufacturer's instructions carefully. Read them through once or twice before you begin, if you feel that you are making a mistake or going off course, simply stop, relax, and start again.

● Keep tools clean, and make sure that you use sharp blades and drill bits.

● Never leave a power tool running unattended, even if it's only going to take a moment. Always turn it off.

● Electrical cables can be dangerous, so keep your eyes open and be careful not to trip over them. This is especially true where extension cords are concerned.

● Wear gloves when handling wire or sharp edges.

● Use adhesives carefully. Follow the instructions on the package and make sure that you select the proper glue for the materials that you are working with. If in doubt, ask someone from your local home improvement store.

● Secure items firmly when cutting or drilling.

● Tie long hair back and remove all loose jewelry. Make sure that your clothes don't hang loosely—roll up your sleeves to work!

● Don't be discouraged by these safety pointers; they are here to help you; most accidents are preventable nine times out of ten, so these safety precautions are worth following.

MDF

MDF (medium-density fiberboard) has become very popular, featured heavily on home improvement shows, and in magazines. It is easy to work with and is relatively inexpensive: its smooth surface is perfect for paint finishes—no wonder it's so popular. It pays to respect your materials, however, so caution should be used when working with it. MDF is made from sawdust bound together by adhesives to form a strong, smooth board. The dust from cutting MDF can be irritating, so always wear a mask and work in a well-ventilated area. The average home woodworker is unlikely to be affected as contact with the dust is relatively minor, but it's a sensible precaution nonetheless.

Measurements

When starting a project, decide to use either imperial or metric measurents, and stick to them. Don't switch between systems, as consistency —and the finished project—will be affected.

Toolbox

This set of tools will get you started. Before you begin a new project, check to make sure that you have all the tools required, so that you have everything on hand—there's nothing more frustrating than having to project halfway through a step because you don't have the necessary equipment.

Invest in a decent-sized toolbox to store all your gear. These boxes are inexpensive and can be found in a variety of sizes.

Finally, take care of your tools. If you keep them clean and dust free, they will last longer and perform well.

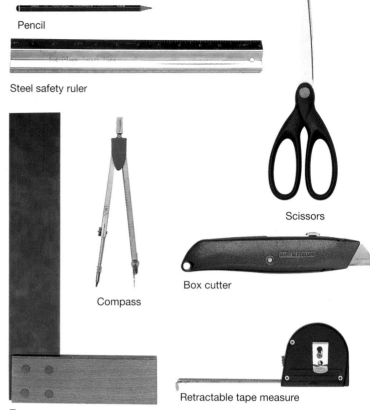

Pencil

Steel safety ruler

Scissors

Box cutter

Compass

Retractable tape measure

Try square

Miter block

Spirit level

Jigsaw

Staple gun

Back saw

Crosscut saw

Hand drill

Flat bit

Straight bit

Countersink bit

Hole saw

Power drill

Pliers

Selection of nails and screws

Corner plates

Flat plate

Nail (center) punch

Bradawl

Wood adhesive

Epoxy resin adhesive

Filler knife

Phillips head screwdriver

Flat head screwdriver

Claw hammer   Pin hammer

Adhesive gun and gap-filling adhesive

Corner clamp

Flat paintbrush

Stippling brush

C-clamp

Artist's brush

Sandpaper in several grades, including wet and dry, with sanding block

Techniques

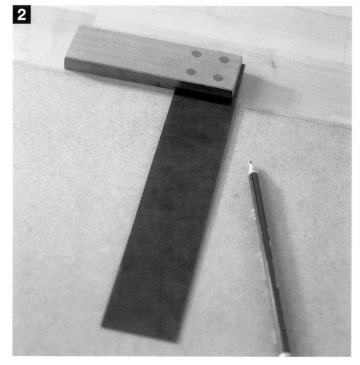

1 Measuring

a) To measure from an edge with a tape measure, hook the end of the tape over the edge to hold it in place and mark the proper measurement with a pencil. For a line parallel to the edge, slide the tape down along the edge and mark again. Get someone to help when measuring long distances.

b) To join measured points, use a steel safety ruler to join rows of pencil marks. Use a soft pencil for drawing lines so the marks can be erased easily.

2 Using a try square to mark parallel lines

This device makes drawing parallel lines a straightforward job. Simply rest the top of the try square over the top edge of the piece that you are working on, and draw a pencil line along the metal edge.

3 Draw diagonals to find the center of a rectangle

To find the true center of a rectangular or square piece of wood, draw two diagonal lines from corner to corner. The point where the lines intersect is the center.

4 Waxing the saw teeth

This helps to lubricate the saw and thus makes the cutting action smoother. Soap is an alternative that works just as well, but be warned—lubricating will only help sharp blades and will not make blunt blades better.

5

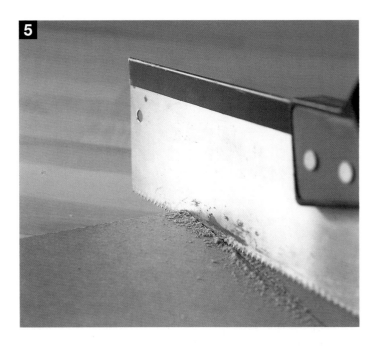

5 Cutting with a back saw
Make one or two cuts to create a small notch before you start cutting. The blade will be more stable and you will do a better job.

6

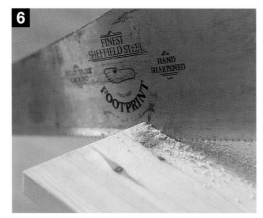

6 Cutting with a crosscut saw
Because a crosscut saw is longer and does not have strengthening along the top, you have to take care that the blade does not flex while you are sawing—practice will pay dividends here.

7

8

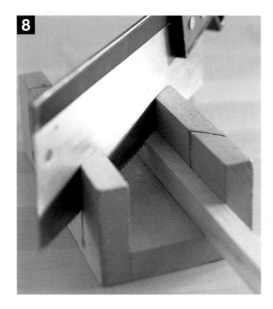

7 Cutting a straight line in a miter block
Miter blocks are an invaluable way of ensuring that a straight line is really straight. Simply slot the saw through the parallel notches on either side and saw down through your length of wood. Clamping a miter block in a workbench gives it extra stability and makes the work easier.

8 Cutting a miter in a miter block
Mitered edges are cut at 45 degrees so they form neat corners when joined together. Use the same principle as cutting straight lines, but this time, slot the blade of the saw through one of the two notches that are diagonally opposite one another.

9 Cutting a wavy line with a jigsaw

If you haven't used a jigsaw before, they behave in much the same way as a sewing machine, but with a blade instead of a needle. The key to accurate cutting is to make sure that the surface is firmly secured (in a workbench, for example)—and to take your time. Simply guide the blade along the line that you have drawn, and if you go off course for any reason, don't panic; stop and restart in the right direction. Minor mistakes can be smoothed away with sandpaper. For the best results, the blade should always be sharp.

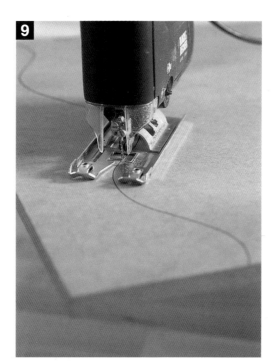

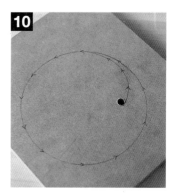

10 Cutting out an internal circle

After drawing the circle, drill a hole a few fractions of an inch away from its edge at the top right. If you are right-handed, you will be cutting from right to left in a counterclockwise direction. If you are left-handed, drill the hole at the top left and cut clockwise.

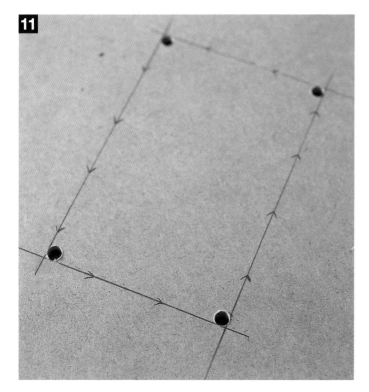

12 Cutting thin dowels

With very narrow dowels, mark the area you want to cut and hold a sharp box cutter blade over the mark. Roll the dowel until it cuts in two. With slightly thicker dowels, use the same method to score the wood, then snap it in two and sand to finish.

11 Cutting out an internal square

Before you start cutting, drill four holes, one at each corner of the square—the holes should sit inside the pencil marks and be wide enough to accommodate the jigsaw's blade. Start at one corner and work along one side until you reach the next corner. You may have to unclamp the wood and rotate it after cutting each side to make it easier to work. Always cut in the same direction.

13 **Cutting recessed hinges**
The surface of rebated hinges should sit flush with the surrounding wood or MDF. Use the hinges themselves as a template and draw around their outline in pencil. With a sharp box cutter, carefully score along these lines, then, working the blade horizontally, remove a fine layer, one at a time until you have reached the correct depth. If you remove too much, you can rectify the mistake by applying a fine layer of filler.

14 **Sanding a flat surface**
A sanding block makes it easier to cover a large area and prevents friction burn. There are several types of block, although they all basically do the same job. Sandpaper comes in different grades. In general, rough grades are used first, followed by finer ones to give a completely smooth finish. Wet and dry paper are used between coats of paint or varnish, almost polishing the surface, making it completely smooth. Always finish with a coat of paint or varnish, however (unless you are distressing a surface) as the action of sanding will affect the finished color. For the best results, apply paint in the same direction as you sanded.

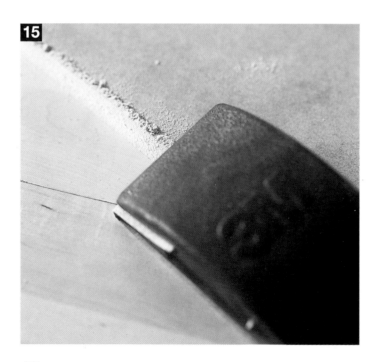

15 **Sanding a rounded edge**
Use the same principle as before, but this time angle the sanding block so that it removes the hard edge of the wood. This is easier if the wood is properly secured.

16 **Sanding a corner**
Again, this technique removes the hard edges, this time at the corner points. This takes little time and is a prudent safety precaution, particularly on lower level items such as benches or tables.

17 Sanding the inside of a circle
Customize a length of dowel or use a pencil wrapped in sandpaper, so that you can easily work it around the diameter of the cut circle.

18 Using a bradawl
This tool ensures accuracy whether you are fixing screws or nails, or making a pilot hole for a fine drill bit. Find and mark the exact center of the hole and firmly dig in the pointed end of the bradawl. This will give you a good starting point.

19 Drilling a hole
Mark the exact center of the hole that you want to drill with a pencil. Hold the drill perpendicular to the surface so that you are not drilling at an angle. If the bit has a point, ensure that this sits on the center of the mark before you start to drill. Start with a fine drill bit and work your way up if necessary. For the best results, make sure that you get your full weight behind the drill.

20 Putting tape on a drill bit
If you wish to drill through wood to a specified depth, rather than all the way through, simply measure from the point of the bit to your required depth, and bind the area beyond with masking tape. Drill slowly, and stop when the tape is flush with the surface of the wood, as you will have reached the correct level.

21 Countersinking a screw

Do this on surfaces where it is important that screw holes are not visible. A countersink bit creates a hole with sloped sides into which the countersink screw fits, with its head below the surface of the wood.

23 Screwing two pieces of wood together

Check that you have the correct size of screw for the job before you start. It should be long enough to comfortably fit through the top layer and at least half of the bottom layer of wood.

22 Filling a countersunk screw head

a) The sunken screw head sits with its head a little way below the surface of the wood.

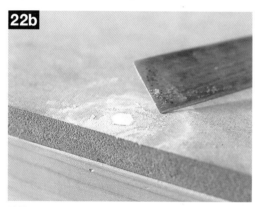

b) The small gap can be filled with wood filler. Smoothed over to the level of the wood. If you are not using galvanized screws, dab a touch of white glue or oil-based paint on the head before applying filler to prevent rusting.

c) When dry, simply sand the filler with very fine paper so that the original hole is virtually undetectable.

24 Nailing two pieces of wood together

a) Check that you have the right nails for the job before you start. Too short and they will not be secure; too long and they will come through the other side of the wood. When in doubt, check your local home improvement or lumber stores.

b) The nail should be hammered in straight. Use a hammer that is a comfortable weight and not too heavy for the size of the nails that you are using.

25 Holding a nail with paper

With smaller nails in particular, it can be tricky getting started without hammering your fingers! If you push the nail through a length of paper or index card, you can hold it steady a few fractions of an inch away and do the job from a safe distance.

26 Punching a nail

For a neat finish, use a nail (center) punch to drive the head of the nail down below the surface of the wood. Hold the punch perpendicular to the nail and drive it in using a hammer. Fill the hole like you would for a countersunk screw head.

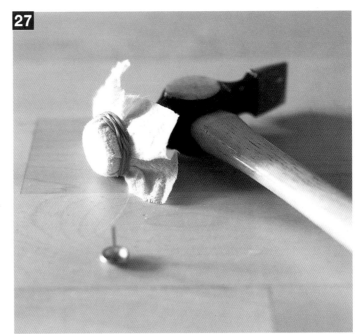

27 Covering a hammer

When hammering upholstery tacks or anything with a decorative head that might get damaged, wrap your hammer with a scrap of soft fabric. Secure it with a length of cord or a rubber band.

28 Glue
Always follow the instructions on the adhesive that you buy, as some will vary.
a) Apply glue to one or both of the sides to be joined (this may depend on the type of glue you use).
b) Use clamps to firmly secure the two pieces that are being joined.
c) Remove any glue that has squeezed out from the join with a cloth immediately—before it has a chance to harden.

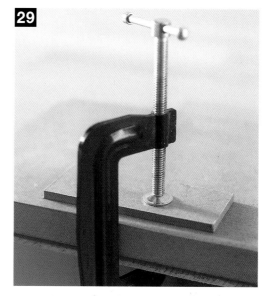

29 Clamping and protecting surfaces
Clamping is a very effective method of holding joints firmly while glue dries, but the clamps' hard metal surfaces can sometimes damage the wood when applied with pressure. To prevent this from happening, particularly on soft wood like pine, simply slot in a thin offcut of wood or MDF to cushion.

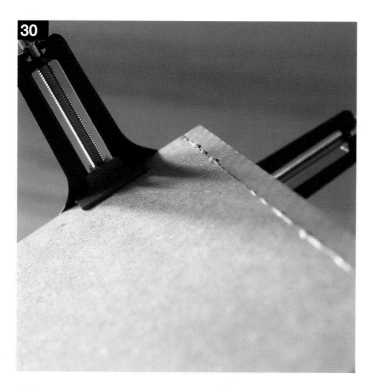

30 Glue and fasten
For the strongest result, metal mending plates like these should be used to press both sides together, for a perfect match. Do not worry about glue working its way out of the join; simply wipe it off.

31 Masking for stripes
Masking tape guarantees a neat, professional edge to any paint finish and is the ideal way of creating perfect stripes. Mark out in pencil where you want the stripes to go. Then run masking tape along the marks' length, checking that the tape edge aligns exactly with the pencil line. Press down firmly all the way down to remove air bubbles before starting to paint. It is easiest to work one color at a time, so make sure that you have masked off the correct stripes. Masking tape is available in several thicknesses, so choose one that's right for the project and the size of your brush.

The Hall

Hallways give the first impression of your home, yet a lack of space can make them a problem to furnish and decorate. A few essential furniture items, combined with a clever color scheme, however, will ensure that your hall gives a warm welcome, whatever its size.

Console table

Few people have the luxury of a spacious hallway, so hall furniture must earn its place. This compact console is no exception. Customized from a set of wooden drawers available from discount furniture stores, this table takes up little space, yet is large enough for a few essential items. You can also adapt the design to make consoles for bedrooms or bathrooms.

you will need

- 1 standard two drawer box
- 1 piece softwood 26¾ x ⅞ x ⅝ in. (680 x 22 x 15mm)
- 2 metal legs with circular brackets and screws
- Miter block
- Handsaw
- Wood glue
- C-clamps
- Power drill and flat bit
- Screws
- Screwdriver
- Jigsaw
- 2 pieces ⅝ in. (15mm) MDF the same diameter as leg brackets
- Bradawl
- 2 handles
- Pearl-finish paint or emulsion paint plus pearl-effect top coat
- Masking tape
- Wall plugs and screws

1 Use the miter block and handsaw to miter the ends of the softwood so that it measures 26¾ in. (680mm) at its longest point. This forms the batten that is fitted to the base of the console table and attaches it to the wall.

2

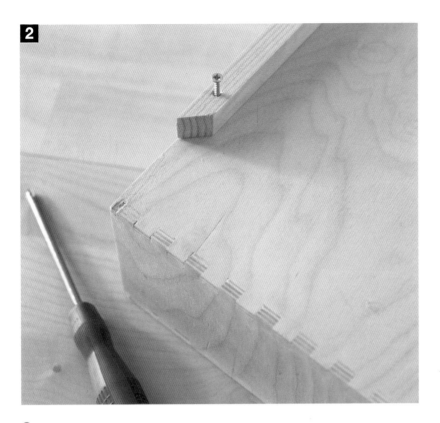

2 Turn the drawers upside down, place the batten against the back edge of the base and mark the ends so that it sits exactly in the middle. Drill three equally spaced pilot holes through the batten, turn to the next face and drill three more equally spaced holes for the wall screws—make sure that the two sets of holes are not too near each other. Apply glue to the batten and clamp it into place. Drive screws into the base. When the glue is dry, remove the clamps.

3

3 Use the metal bracket that attaches the leg to the table as a template to cut out two MDF circles. It is necessary to build up a little extra depth like this, otherwise the screws would drive through the wood into the drawer, making it impossible to open. Sand the circle edges smooth.

4

4 Apply a strong wood adhesive to the MDF circles and position them on the base of the table, one at each corner—the edge of the circles should be around ⅜–¾ in. (10–19mm) from the edges of the base. Secure with clamps and allow to dry.

5

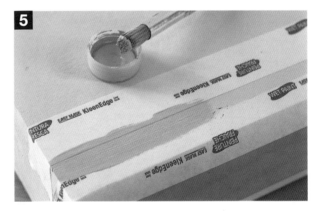

5 Paint the box with two coats of emulsion, making sure that the first coat is completely dry before starting the second. Turn the drawers around so that they have a complete front—to prevent them from sticking, it is best to paint only the front part of the drawers and leave the sides unfinished. To give guidelines for painting a decorative striped border around the edge, apply masking tape to give a ½ in. (12mm) wide line around ¾ in. (19mm) in from the front and back edges. Paint and leave to dry before repeating the process on the two shorter edges. Repeat, this time with a narrower line in a contrasting color.

6 Position the leg brackets on the MDF circles on the base, and use a bradawl to mark the screw holes. Drill holes and use the screws provided in the kit to fasten the circular metal leg bracket onto the MDF.

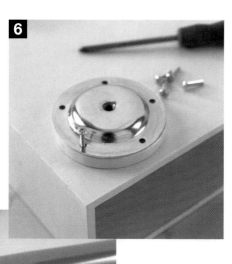

design tips

● You might like to adapt this basic idea to create a small-scale dresser. Simply hang a mirror on the wall behind. Don't be tempted to amass clutter, as the table isn't strong enough to bear much weight.

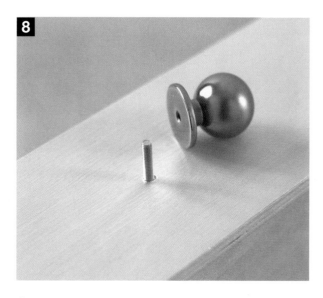

7 Attach the legs, following the instructions on the kit. With an assistant, carefully position the finished table against the wall so that the legs are square on the ground. Mark a horizontal line on the wall, using the underside of the batten as a guide, check it with a spirit level. Use the pilot holes in the batten to mark for wall plugs, then remove the table. Drill and insert the wall plugs, then reposition the table and drive in the wall screws through the batten.

8 Drill any necessary holes, then screw a handle into the painted front of each drawer to complete your console table.

For a glamorous finish, use a specialized paint that gives a pearly luster. You can even experiment with using both plain and pearly finishes.

Radiator cover

A lot more fun—both to look at and make—than the average radiator cover. The basic construction is straightforward, but if you are new to working with wood, it is best to start on a relatively small size. Once you feel confident, why not experiment with different finishing touches on the front panel to give your radiator cover a really unique look?

dimensions

No dimensions have been given for the pieces here, as they will obviously vary based on the size of the radiator that you wish to cover. Measure it carefully, taking note of any valves and pipes, and remember to include the depth—how far out from the wall it stands. When you have completed your measurements, add ⅜–¾ in. (10–19mm) all around so that the cover stands apart from the surface of the radiator. Pipework usually runs close to the wall and doesn't present much of a problem. You will need easy access to valves—cutting a small section out of the side is usually the simplest way to reach the valve.

FRONT
- 1 piece MDF

SIDES
- 2 pieces MDF

TOP
- 1 piece MDF
- 2 softwood battens
- Jigsaw
- Power drill, hole saw, and flat bits
- Sandpaper
- Steel ruler

- Pencil
- Compasses
- Bradawl
- Metal studs
- Hammer, with fabric to cover head
- Screws for battens
- Corner braces with short screws
- Screwdriver
- Gloss paint and primer (optional)
- Emulsion paint and water-based varnish (optional)

1 Mark two sections along the base edge of the front piece to form legs, using a pair of compasses to create curves. The measurements and the number of legs will depend on the size of your radiator. If you aren't sure what will look best, experiment on a cardboard template. For a long radiator like the one shown here, a central leg is a good idea; on smaller radiators, side legs alone are fine. The height of the legs should be roughly one-fifth to one-sixth the overall height of the radiator. Draw a pencil line on the front piece of MDF, parallel to the base, making sure that the base of the radiator will not show. Use a jigsaw to cut out the section or sections and sand the cut edge until it is smooth.

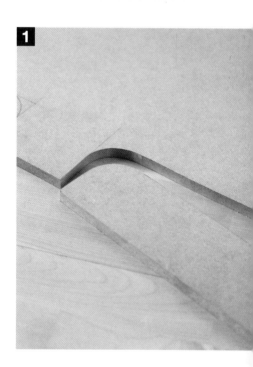

2 Use different size hole saw attachments on a power drill to cut random holes in the front piece, working from the outer face inward. If you aren't sure about how the pattern will look, plot it out on graph paper before you start. Alternatively, stick round pieces of paper of various sizes on the MDF and move them around to give you an idea. Sand the edges of the holes.

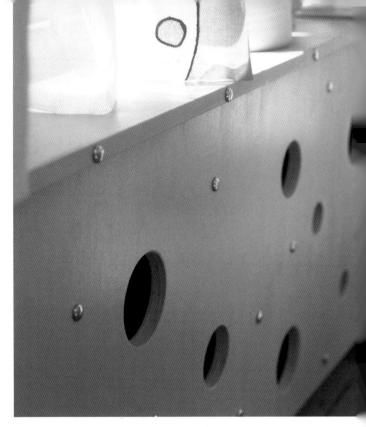

3 Gently sand, dust, and paint the front, side, and top pieces. You can either use primer and an oil-based paint such as eggshell or gloss, or emulsion paint with an oil-based varnish on top. Allow to dry completely.

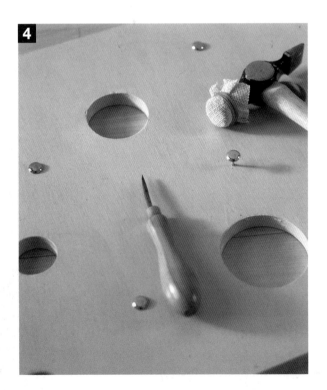

4 To further decorate the front piece, use a bradawl to make small random pilot holes for metal studs. Before driving in the studs, cover the hammer head with a piece of fabric as shown, to avoid damaging the stud heads.

design tips

● Decorative, yet practical, wire meshes and grills are perfect for radiator covers. Alternatively, for a more rustic look, you can try gardener's chicken wire, which comes in a variety of gauges and is inexpensive.

5 Repeat step 4 for the front edge of the top piece, this time making the pilot holes at regular intervals. To prevent the wood from splitting, you can enlarge the bradawl holes with a small drill bit before hammering in the studs.

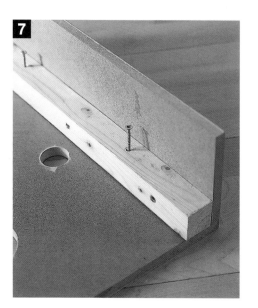

7 Position the sides and battens against the front piece as shown, and repeat step 6 to attach the sides to the front. Again, make sure that the screws you use are long enough to go through the batten and into the front, but not so long that they break out on the other side.

6 The softwood battens that attach the sides to the front are the same length as the side pieces of MDF. Mark and drill regularly spaced guide holes through the battens; the screws used must be long enough to bite into the sides without breaking through the outer face. Lay one side down onto its painted face, position a batten so its edge is exactly along the side edge, and drive in the screws through the guide holes. Repeat for the other batten and side piece.

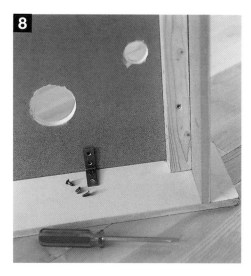

8 Lay the top piece on its painted side. Position the assembled sides and front in place, then position corner braces to hold the front and top together at regular intervals along the meeting edges—again, the number of plates depends on the size of the cover. Mark and bradawl the screw holes through the plates, then drive in very short, stubby screws that do not protrude through the MDF.

Once you have got the hang of the basic construction of the radiator cover, there is no end to the effects you can create on the front panel. A simple grid of rectangular shapes in varying widths, backed with muslin, can look extremely effective.

Letter rack

Every hall should have a handy letter rack to help prevent papers and keys from getting lost. Don't be discouraged by the number of steps—it is quite simple to make, although you will need to work methodically as some of the techniques are a bit complicated. If you prefer to change the shape of the rack, all you need do is draw your own template. When your rack is complete, you'll wonder how you ever lived without it.

you will need

- 1 piece ½ in. (12mm) MDF 39 x 13⅜ in. (990 x 340 mm)
- Steel ruler
- 1 piece paper 13⅜ x 6 in. (340 x 150mm)
- Box cutter
- Small back saw
- Pencil
- Dressmaker pins
- Sliding bevel
- Try square
- 2 pieces softwood 27¼ x 1¼ x ⅞ in. (690 x 33 x 22mm)
- Wood glue
- C-clamps
- Brads
- 3 lengths ⅜ in. (10mm) diameter dowel 17⅜ in. (440mm) long
- Power drill and ⅜ in. (10mm) flat bit
- Emulsion paint
- Sandpaper
- Fine beading

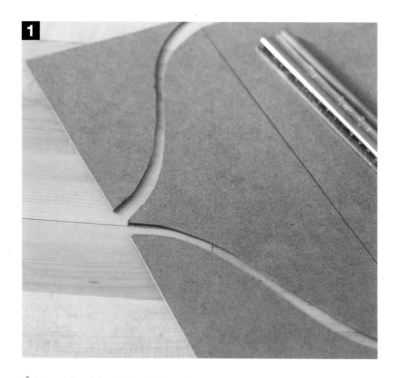

1 Draw a line 6 in. (150mm) down from—and parallel to—the top of the hardboard. Repeat at the base. To make a template, fold the piece of paper in half lengthwise and trace half of the curved design from the diagram onto it (see Templates). Cut along the line that you have drawn, open the paper out, and place it in position on the hardboard with the steel ruler on the pencil line. Draw around the paper shape at the top and base, and use a sharp box cutter to cut out the design.

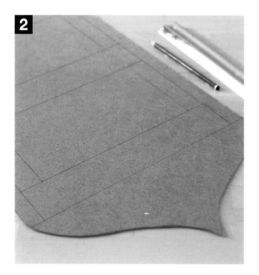

2 You need to measure the hardboard and create a grid of pencil lines to act as a guide for the three flaps. This isn't difficult, just a little time-consuming—use a try square to ensure that the lines are parallel. Don't be tempted to rush the job: the old adage "Measure twice and cut once" is the best guide.

3 The three inner rectangles that you have drawn will form the flaps in which you can store letters and papers. With a box cutter, cut along the top edge and two sides of each of the three flaps. Leave the base lines intact.

4 Stick a dressmakers' pin through each of the corners where the cut side lines join the base of the flaps. Make sure that the points emerge on the other side. The pins will provide you with an accurate guide for the next step.

design tips
● To disguise the cracked hardboard at the base of each flap, cut a very fine length of beading to the width of the rack and glue it in place.

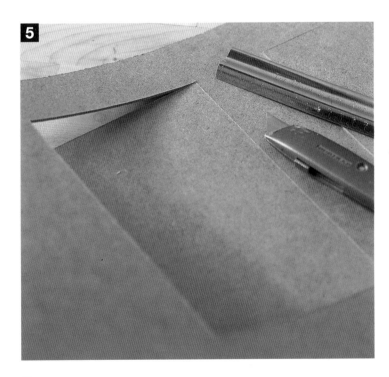

5 Turn the hardboard over so that the back of the rack faces upward. You should be able to see the sharp ends of two pins sticking through at the base of each flap. Score lightly with a box cutter between these two points to break the outer layer of board enabling the flap to pull forward slightly. Repeat for each flap and then remove the pins.

6 Cut to length two battens to run down either side of the rack and hold the lengths of dowel. Set a sliding bevel to an angle over 45 degrees and draw this angle on each end of both battens, ensuring that all the angles are the same. Use the back saw to cut the ends, and smooth them with sandpaper.

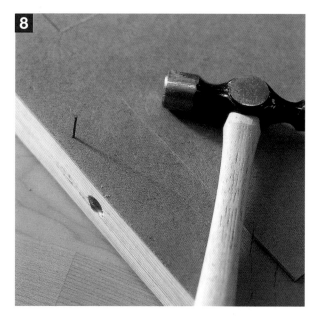

8 Clean up the holes with sandpaper. Glue and clamp the battens in place and, from the back of the hardboard, hammer brads in to secure the joins. Allow to dry.

7 Place one of the battens flat in position on the MDF rack. Measure 2 in. (50mm) up from the base of each flap and mark this accurately on the batten in pencil. These marks form the center points of the holes for the dowel. Sandwich the battens together to ensure that the holes line up, then drill through each of the pencil marks using a flat bit.

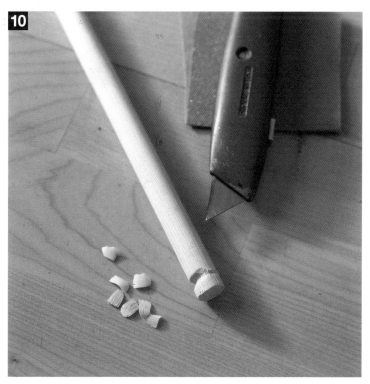

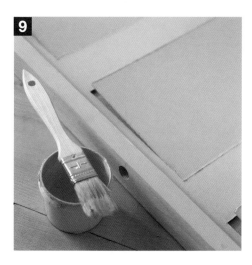

9 Lightly sand and dust the whole rack and then paint it, including the edges of the hardboard, with emulsion. Remember to paint the inside of the flaps for a smart finish. Allow to dry.

10 Make a pencil mark for the notches around ⅜ in. (10mm) in from either end of each length of the dowels. Carefully score a fine line along the mark with a box cutter, then cut out a V-shaped notch with the knife until you have an indentation all around. Smooth the whole length of dowel lightly with fine sandpaper. Slide the lengths of dowel through the holes.

The Living Room

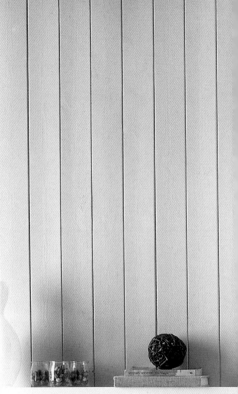

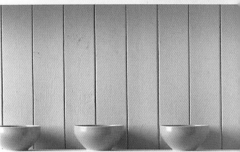

One of the most public rooms in the house—and the most versatile—the living room may be used for entertaining friends, relaxing with a good book, or simply unwinding in front of the television. All this can make choosing furniture a tall order. Comfort and function are equally important—not forgetting style. The simple pieces on the following pages not only look good, but will prove extremely useful too. Like all classic designs, they will never date: simply repaint them for a fresh, new look when you want to make changes.

Fireplace

Traditionally, the hearth has always been the heart of the home. In many older homes, however, fireplaces have either been boarded over or removed altogether, and many modern homes were built without fireplaces. This elegant surround will help reinstate a focal point in your living room—even if you don't have a real fire, you can create a stunning display with candles or flowers—and although it is a large project, it is remarkably easy to make. Take it a step at a time, and enlist the help of friends.

you will need

Inner section
- Two pieces wood or MDF 27½ x 8 x ¾ in. (700 x 200 x 19mm)
- One piece wood or MDF 35½ x 11¾ x ¾ in. (900 x 300 x 19mm)

Outer section
- Two pieces wood or MDF 47¼ x 8 x ¾ in. (1200 x 200 x 19mm)
- One piece wood or MDF 31½ x 11¾ x ¾ in. (800 x 300 x 19mm)

Sides
- Two pieces wood or MDF 47¼ x 4 x ¾ in. (1200 x 100 x 19mm)

Mantel shelf
- (Top) One piece wood or MDF 50¼ x 7½ x ¾ in. (1275 x 190 x 19mm)
- (Front) One piece wood or MDF 51¼ x 2 x ¾ in. (1300 x 50 x 19mm)
- (Sides) Two pieces wood or MDF 7½ x 2 x ¾ in. (190 x 50 x 19mm)
- Bradawl
- Screwdriver
- Countersunk wood screws ½ x ⅛ in. (12 x 4mm)
- Eight 5 in. (125mm) mending plates
- Wood glue
- Emulsion paint
- Oil-based paint
- Corner clamps
- Fine nails
- Center punch
- Wood filler
- Sandpaper
- Hammer

1 The fireplace is formed from two inverted U shapes with a mantel shelf along the top. To make the inner U section, lay the two short pieces (the legs) against the long one, setting the long one across the top of the shorter pair. Make sure the side edges meet exactly, then place two flat plates across each joint, angled for strength. Use a bradawl to mark the screw holes. Apply glue to the joining edges, position them accurately, and screw the meeting plates in place. Leave to dry.

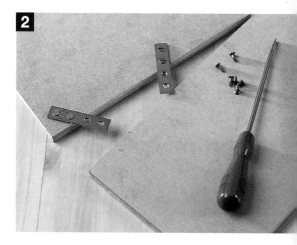

2 Now make the outer section—this time, the middle piece slots in between the two legs instead of lying along the top of them. Lay out the pieces as before, this time making sure that there is at least a 5 in. (125mm) gap between the bottom of the middle section and the flat plates, to allow for the inner section when the two frames are joined together. Apply glue, drive in the screws, and leave to dry.

3 Before you join the outer and inner sections together to create the front of the fireplace, you need to make sure that the sections fit squarely onto one another. Lay the inner section on its back, then measure 2 in. (50mm) in from the outer edges and mark this along each leg. Join the marks to make a line along each leg.

4 Now line up the inner edges of the outside section with the marks that you have just drawn on the inner frame. Check carefully that both sections are square, then apply glue all around the three edges where the inner and outer sections overlap. Fit the sections together and allow to dry. *Inset:* When the glue has dried, countersink fine nails at 4 in. (100mm) intervals along the inner edge of the outer section. Use a center punch to push the nail heads below the surface of the wood, then fill the holes with a little wood filler. Allow to dry, then sand the filler smooth with the wood surface.

design tips

● To avoid confusion when assembling the sections, mark each piece of wood for the section that it is intended for.

● Unless you are very adept, ask your local lumber merchant to cut the wood for you. Avoid as much wastage as possible.

● If you are making the surround to fit a specific opening, you will have to modify the dimensions. If in doubt, trace the pieces onto large sheets of brown paper before you start ordering or cutting wood.

● Wooden battens or metal brackets are the most common methods of securing fireplaces to a wall, but the best method will depend on the material from which your wall is built. Check with your local hardware store for advice on specific materials and securing methods.

● You can create a hearth from wood, slate, or marble. Consult your local home improvement store.

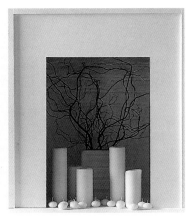

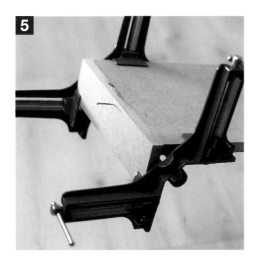

5 Select the two narrow side pieces and check that they are an exact fit along the edges of the outer sections. Glue them into position as shown, and secure with corner clamps. When dry, secure the join with nails from the front, then punch the nails down, fill, and sand as before.

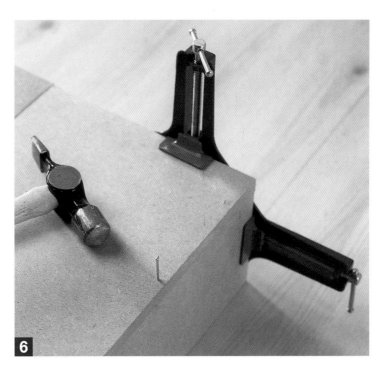

6 The shelf section is made from four pieces of wood—a top, front, and two sides. Check to make sure that the sides fit on the outside edges of the shelf, then apply glue; position the sides and clamp them in place. Nail, punch down, fill, and sand as before.

7 When the top and sides are dry, position them on their back edges and check the front for fit. Attach it in the same way as before. This time you will not be able to use corner clamps, but you should be able to manage without as long as you work carefully at each stage of the process.

8 Place the mantel shelf in position on the main frame, making sure that there is a 2 in. (50mm) overhang at either end. center the shelf, apply glue and clamp it in place. Drive three nails on either side through the shelf top into the frame side pieces. Punch the nails down to countersink them, then fill and sand as before. Fill and sand any gaps in the finished fireplace, then prime with emulsion and use an oil-based paint.

Display boxes

Once you get the hang of making these handy little display boxes, you won't want to stop—and it is easy to see why. Each box does not take long to make and can be painted and repainted to go with any color scheme. The boxes look great mounted on the wall, either individually or in groups or rows, showing off your favorite possessions. They also make great gifts for family and friends.

you will need

SIDES
- 2 pieces MDF
  8 x 6 x ⅝ in.
  (200 x 150 x 15mm)

TOP AND BASE
- 2 pieces MDF
  6¾ x 6 x ⅝in.
  (170 x 150 x 15mm)
- Wood glue
- Corner clamps
- Sandpaper and
  sanding block
- Steel ruler
- Pencil
- Hammer
- Fine nails
- center punch
- Wood filler
- Emulsion paint
- Water-based
  varnish

1 Dry assemble the box on its back with the top and base held inside its sides. Mark the meeting edges and outer faces of all four of the pieces.

Before putting the pieces together, chamfer the outer edges of the top and bottom sections along the depth of the box. This helps to mask any slight inaccuracy in the finished, shaped pieces.

2 Apply glue along the top inside end of one side piece, then position it and the meeting edge of the top piece together in a "L" shape, holding them in place with corner clamps until completely dry. Repeat with the other side piece, this time with the glue along the bottom meeting edge

design tips

- As these boxes are quite small, they are an excellent way of using up leftover paint.
- When you get the hang of making the boxes, you can experiment with different dimensions. Don't be tempted to make them too big—they work best on a small scale.

3 Use a ruler and pencil to mark a line across the sides, ⁵⁄₁₆ in. (8mm) from each end. Mark for three equally spaced nails along each of these lines. Hammer in fine nails to strengthen the glued joints, then glue, assemble, and clamp the two "L" shaped pieces together to create a square box. Allow to dry, then hammer in nails to strengthen the "new" joints.

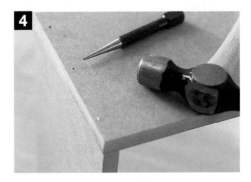

4 Use a center punch and hammer to push down the heads of the nails so that they lie below the surface of the MDF. Fill the holes with wood filler, allow to dry and sand smooth. Paint the boxes with emulsion, allow to dry, and finish with a couple of coats of water-based varnish.

Coffee table

Whether you want to make this table from scratch or prefer to customize an existing one, by incorporating test tubes into the design, you will never have to look for a vase again!

The simplest ideas really are the best. A plain table has been given a contemporary twist with the addition of nine drilled holes and a set of glass test tubes (available from pharmaceutical suppliers). Presto! An instant new look—and one that can be changed as often as you change a floral arrangement (you can also use dried flowers). Take time in deciding how many holes you want—and where you want to position them. You might prefer a more random effect or perhaps a wavy line, bisecting the table diagonally from corner to corner. Your imagination is the limit. Once you have plotted exactly where you want to drill, mark each spot carefully. Err on the side of caution: it is easy to make a small hole slightly larger, but impossible to tighten a hole that has been drilled too big.

you will need

Top
- 1 piece MDF 26⅝ x 26⅝ x ¾ in. (675 x 675 x 19mm)

Rails
- 4 pieces softwood 21 x 1¾ x ¾ in. (535 x 45 x 19mm)
- 8 right-angle brackets 1½ x 1⅛ x 1 in. (38 x 30 x 25mm)
- 32 woodscrews ½ in. (12mm) long

Legs
- 4 pieces softwood 17 x 1¾ x 1¾ in. (430 x 45 x 45mm)
- 8 right-angle brackets 1½ x 1⅛ x ⅜ in. (38 x 30 x 10mm)
- 32 woodscrews ⅝ in. (16mm) long
- 9 glass ¾ in. (19mm) diameter test tubes
- Straightedge
- Pencil
- Hand saw or jigsaw
- Power drill and ¾ in. (19mm) flat bit
- Bradawl
- Screwdriver
- Try square
- Wood glue
- Corner clamps
- Sandpaper and sanding block
- Primer and emulsion or gloss paint

1 Cut the table top to size with a crosscut saw or jigsaw, making sure that the corners are true right angles. Find the center of of the top by drawing corner-to-corner diagonals, then measure and draw edge-to-edge lines through the center in both directions. Draw two more lines, 2¾ in. (70mm) on either side of one horizontal line. Where these lines meet the diagonals, join them to make a square.

2 Where the lines intersect, use a ¾ in. (19mm) flat bit to drill a hole at each meeting point. Sand the insides of the nine holes, check that an ¾ in. (19mm) diameter test tube will fit, and adjust the holes as required.

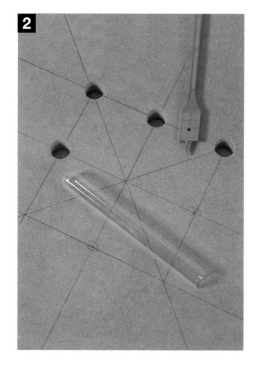

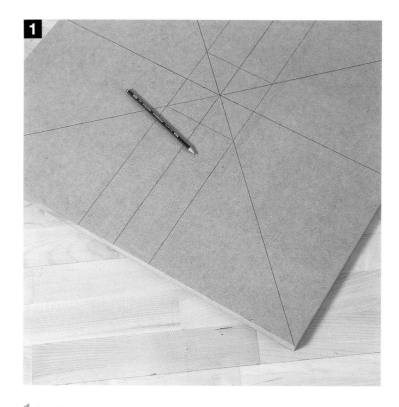

3 Cut the four rails to length, ensuring that the ends are cut square. Measure and mark 3⅜ in. (85mm) from each end. Hold a rail bracket with its outer edge against each mark in turn, with the 1⅛ in. (30mm) edge against the wood, and use a bradawl to make pilot screw holes—it is vital that the "L" is flush with the bottom edge of the rail. Screw the bracket in place, using the ½ in. (12mm) long woodscrews.

4 On the bottom face of the table top, use a try square to mark 2¾ in. (70mm) from each end at the corners, and a straightedge to mark a line 1⅝ in. (40mm) in from, and parallel to, each edge. Position each rail in turn with the outside edges on the lines, bradawl pilot holes, and screw into place—use a try square to check that the rails meet the top at right angles.

5 Cut the legs to length, and make sure that both ends are cut square. Apply wood glue to one end of a leg and each end of two rails at a corner. Push the leg to meet the rails, and use corner clamps to hold it in place, checking the right angle between leg and top with a try square. Repeat for the other legs and leave to dry completely.

design tips

● You can use gloss or emulsion paints for a solid color finish to match your room.
● Use your imagination to create other finishes—combining colors, painting stripes or patterns, using spray paints, and so on.

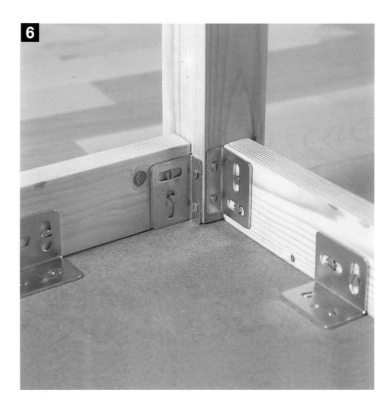

6 Hold a leg bracket against the leg and rail with the narrow edge on the leg, then bradawl pilot holes. Stagger the other bracket for that leg as shown, so that the screws do not hit each other. Screw the brackets in place, using the ⅝ in. (16mm) long woodscrews. Repeat for the other legs. To finish, prime and paint the table, and when dry, slide the test tubes into the holes in the top.

Tall shelves

The neat proportions of this shelving unit make it ideal for slipping
into awkward spaces that you otherwise may not use. A design
classic, the shelves are easy both to make and easy to live with. They
look elegant standing upright, and can also be turned sideways to create
a low-level unit that doubles as a coffee table. Keep the finish simple
with an understated color that allows the grain of the wood
to show through.

design tips

- Because it can be difficult to cut a true
  straight line on large pieces like these with
  a hand-held saw, you may prefer to ask
  your local lumber merchant to cut the
  pineboard for you.
- These shelves can be fastened to the wall
  for extra stability if required—in children's
  rooms, for example. Use flat brass plates,
  screws, and wall plugs.

you will need

SIDES
- 2 pieces pineboard 69 x 12⅜ x ¾ in.
  (1755 x 315 x 19mm)

TOP, BASE, AND SHELVES
- 4 pieces pine 17¼ x 12⅜ x ¾ in.
  (437 x 315 x 19mm)
- Corner clamps
- Wood glue
- Power drill with countersink bit
- Countersunk screws
- Screwdriver
- Pencil
- Steel ruler
- Wood filler
- Sandpaper
- Brass plates, screws, and wall plugs
  (optional)
- Four casters (optional)
- Woodstain
- Matte varnish

1

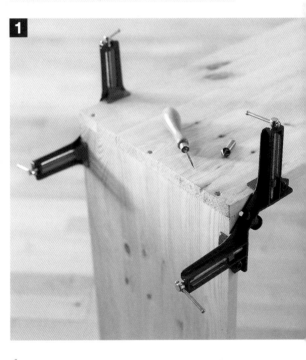

1 Lay one of the side pieces flat and at one end stand a smaller piece on top and at right angles to it. Apply wood glue to the meeting edges of both pieces and secure with a corner clamp— you will have to up-end the "L" shaped piece and support the opposite end on a low table or pile of books until the glue has dried thoroughly. Drill three equally spaced pilot holes and countersink screws through the end piece and into the side piece to secure the joint. Repeat for the opposite end using the same method. Allow the glue to dry, then remove the clamps.

2

alternative ideas

- The shelves can be turned on their side and used as a low storage unit and coffee table in one. Simply screw on casters at each corner so that the unit is easy to move around the room.
- You might like to make a set of shelves on a smaller scale than this, as a specific piece of storage, for videos or magazines for example. Make sure that you choose casters that are an appropriate scale for the design.
- The design could easily be adapted to work as a television and video unit or as a low-level divider for a room where two children are sharing. To make it extra safe, invest in casters that incorporate a locking device.

2 To work out the position of the two shelves, measure the inside length of the sides and divide the figure by three. Mark these measurements accurately in pencil on the front and back faces of the sides. Before you fit the shelves, mark half the thickness of each one on the front and back. These marks should align with the pencil marks on the frame. Apply glue to the ends of the shelves and secure them in place with miter clamps—this will be easier if you stand the piece on its "legs," as if it was a low table. Continue the pencil line from the shelves across the faces of the side, mark and drill three equally spaced pilot holes. Countersink screw holes and drive in the screws.

3 To attach the second side, apply glue to the edges of the shelves, top, and base and place the side in position. Make sure that you line up the center pencil marks. Secure with corner clamps. When the glue has dried thoroughly, remove the clamps, mark drill holes, and countersink three screws through the top and base of each shelf as before. Fill all the screw holes with wood filler, allow to dry, and sand smooth with the wood surface.

Hinged
mirror

The opulent finish on this mirror
gives it an expensive, designer look
that is irresistibly glamorous. The
metal leaf that creates the
shimmering effect is tricky to handle,
but the end result is unparalleled.

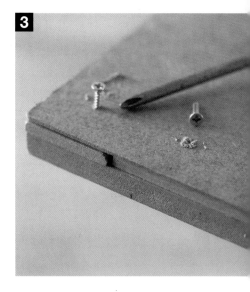

1 To secure the mirror to the hardboard backing, pack it into position with four packing strips. Do not use glue to stick the mirror directly onto the board, as not all types of adhesive are compatible with the materials you are using, and may react with the mirror. Lay the mirror in place, then apply glue to the bare backing and position the top strip, the sides, and the bottom piece. Use clamps or heavy weights to hold the packing until the glue is dry.

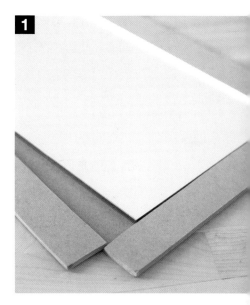

2 Use a pencil and steel ruler to mark the rectangular cutout hole for the mirror on the frame piece of MDF—this should be about ⅜ in. (10mm) smaller than the mirror, i.e. 17½ x 9¾ in. (450 x 250mm). Drill holes in each of the four corners, to give the jigsaw a clean starting point. Smooth the rough edges with sandpaper.

3 Position the mirror assembly against the back of the frame, then carefully lay both pieces face down on a flat surface, with the backing now on the top. To keep the three sections sandwiched together firmly, you will need to attach a couple of screws in each corner. Measure carefully, to make sure that you do not crack the glass, then drill or bradawl small pilot holes. Use ⅝ in. (15mm) screws so as not to come through the front of the frame. Fill any gaps where the packing strips meet one another, with a little wood filler, and sand smooth when dry.

4

4 To make the doors, measure 2⅜ in. (60mm) in from the top right corner and the same distance in from the bottom left of the other large piece of MDF. Draw a line between the two points with a steel rule and pencil, and cut along the line with a jigsaw. Sand any rough edges. Lay the frame right side up and place one door on either side, as they would be if opened out. Open the hinges flat, and position them equally and identically on both sides, with one half on the door and the other half on the frame. Draw around the hinges and use a box cutter to cut shallow rabbets so that the four hinges are flush against the MDF.

you will need

FRAME AND DOORS
● 2 pieces MDF 22¼ x 14⅜ x ½in. (565 x 365 x 12mm)
BACKING
● 1 pieces hardboard 22¼ x 14⅜in. (565 x 365mm)
PACKING STRIPS
● 2 pieces MDF 14¼ x 2 x ½in. (360 x 50 x 12mm)
● 2 pieces MDF 18 x 2 x ½in. (460 x 50 x 12mm)
● Mirror 18 x 10¼ in. (460 x 260mm)
● Power drill with straight bit
● 4 flush hinges, 2 in. (50mm) long, with screws
● 2 picture hanging plates and picture wire
● Gilder's tamping brush or cotton wool
● 2 cuphooks with cord or chain
● Wood filler
● Sandpaper
● Jigsaw
● Box cutter
● Screwdriver
● Clear oil varnish
● C-clamps
● white glue for wood
● Steel rule and pencil
● Bradawl
● Masking tape
● Size brush
● Metal leaf and size
● Clear oil varnish
● Tack cloth
● Size

5

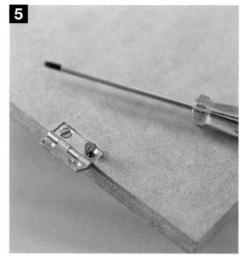

5 Work carefully when cutting the rabbets, so you don't go too deep. Tidy up the rabbets, then position the hinges and use a bradawl to make pilot holes for the screws. Screw the hinges securely to each of the doors.

6

6 Depending on the decorative finish that you plan for the mirror, you can now go one of two ways. If you are going to paint the mirror, screw the other side of the hinge plates to the frame, sand, and apply the paint. If you are planning a more intricate finish or find it easier to work with three small pieces rather than one large one, leave the hinges off the frame for now.

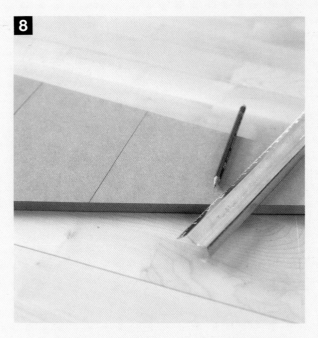

7 Coat all the pieces with a dilute solution of white glue and water, with a ratio of around 3:1, to seal them. Leave to dry thoroughly before starting the next step.

8 Draw pencil lines on the inside and outside of each of the doors to act as a guide for positioning the silver leaf squares. The squares are slightly smaller than the width of the metal leaf itself because the leaves slightly overlap. There's no need to draw guide lines on the frame as it is so narrow. Instead, just use your judgement to line the leaf up with that on the doors.

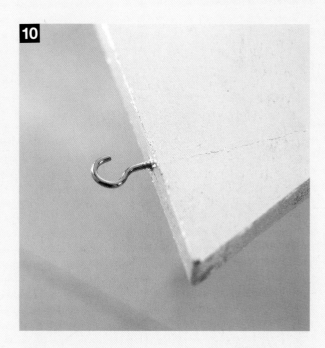

9 You must use a special metal leaf glue to apply the leaves. Other adhesives simply will not work. Traditional glues are oil-based, but newer, water-based types are cleaner and much easier to use. Allow a coat of glue to become tacky and almost dry to the touch. Take a square of metal leaf transfer and apply it face down on the tacky surface. Rub the backing sheet down using a cotton-wool pad or piece of soft cloth. Carefully peel away the backing sheet and blot the leaf with cotton wool. Continue until you have covered the required area.

When the pieces are completely dry, give them a coat or two of an oil-based varnish to seal and protect the delicate surface.

10 Finally, to hold the doors together attach two cup hooks, one to the underside of each of the door. Link these with a length of cord or chain—or anything else that you think looks good.

The Kitchen

No matter what size the kitchen, there never seems to be enough space. But help is at hand in the form of three handy pieces of furniture. For tiny kitchens, start with the smallest project and progress on to the next one when you're ready. You'll be amazed at how good these items look—and the practical difference they will make.

Step stool

Just the right height to help you reach awkward items stored on cupboard tops, this step stool is compact enough to keep in most kitchens or utility rooms. This step stool is not only extremely practical but good-looking too. You'll find hundreds of uses for it.

you will need

SIDES
- 2 pieces MDF 16¾ x 24 x ¾ in. (425 x 405 x 19mm)

STEPS
- 2 pieces softwood 20¼ x 8¼ x 1in. (515 x 210 x 25mm)

BATTENS
- 4 pieces softwood 18⅜ x 1⅛ x 1⅛ in. (470 x 30 x 30mm)
- Jigsaw
- Power drill and straight bit screwdriver
- Wood glue
- Countersunk screws
- Pencil
- Steel ruler
- Compasses
- Sandpaper
- Sanding block
- Emulsion paints

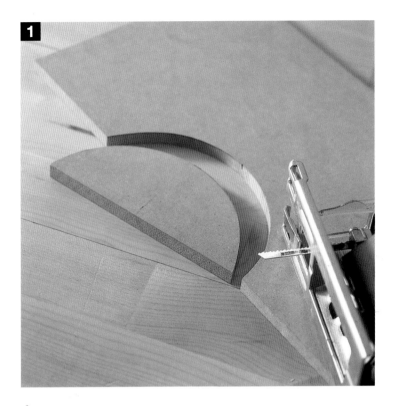

design tips

● To prevent screws from rusting and showing through on the wood surface, dab a spot of oil-based primer on the heads and leave to dry before filling the holes with wood filler.

● To create a distressed finish on the steps, paint them a moderate to dark color and leave this to dry thoroughly. Next, use a lighter colored paint. When this coat has dried, use sandpaper and a sanding block to remove parts of the top coat, leaving areas of the layer underneath to show through. This creates a weathered, aged effect and looks best when used predominantly on edges, where most wear and tear would show.

1 Measure and mark halfway along each edge of one side piece and draw a line from top to bottom and one from side to side. Use a jigsaw to cut out the top right section, which is almost an exact square. Use compasses to mark a curve along the base, with its center over the line already drawn. Use the jigsaw to cut out this shape to form the legs. Repeat on the other side piece, making sure that the two pieces are identical.

2 The four battens help to strengthen the structure. Lay one side on its inner face and position the battens: one at each of the top two corners, one at the front step, and one at the back, just above the curved cutout. Trace around the battens.

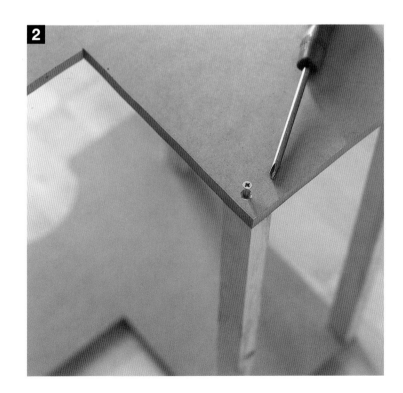

3 Remove the battens and draw diagonal lines between the marked corners of each pencil square on the sides. Drill pilot holes through the MDF where the diagonal lines meet. Apply glue to the batten end, then position it to the drawn square on the inner side face and drive in a countersunk screw through the pilot hole into the batten end. Repeat for all four battens, then repeat the whole process for the other side piece. Allow to dry.

4 Position the bottom step, making sure that the overlap is the same on both sides. Mark and drill pilot holes for two screws through the step into the side frames, then drive in and countersink the screws. Repeat for the top step.

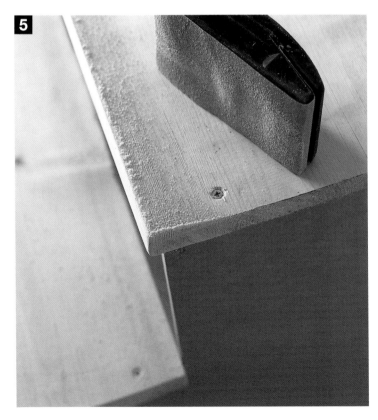

5 To soften the hard angles, chamfer all the edges and corners with sandpaper wrapped around a sanding block—this will also make the stool safer. Fill all countersunk holes with wood filler, leave to dry, and sand smooth.

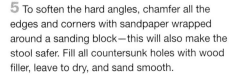

Plate rack

Ideal for storage and display, this handy plate rack is the perfect finishing touch for kitchens. It makes efficient use of available space, and can be customized with the addition of a towel rail or cup hooks. It is heavy, however, so make sure that you get help when fixing it in place.

you will need

BATTENS
- 3 pieces stripwood 24 x 1⅜ x ⅞ in. (610 x 33 x 22mm)

BACK
- 1 piece MDF 31⅝ x 25⅝ x ½ in. (800 x 650 x 12mm)

SIDES
- 2 pieces softwood 45¼ x 12¼ x ¾ in. (1150 x 310 x 19mm)

TOP
- 1 piece softwood 29½ x 12¼ x ¾ in. (748 x 310 x 19mm)

SHELVES
- 2 pieces MDF 23⅝ x 11⅜ x ½ in. (600 x 290 x 12mm)
- 1 piece MDF 23⅝ x 12⅞ x ½ in. (600 x 320 x 12mm)

SHELF SUPPORTS
- 3 pieces quarter dowel 23⅝ in. (600mm) long
- 6 pieces quarter dowel 11 in. (280mm) long
- Pencil
- Screws
- Screwdriver
- Jigsaw
- Sandpaper and sanding block
- Power drill and straight bit
- Miter clamps
- White school glue
- Back saw and miter block
- Hammer
- Brads
- Primer and emulsion or eggshell colored paint

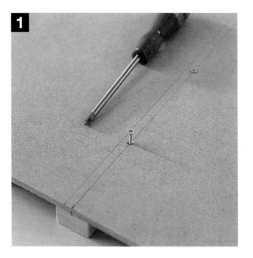

1 On the reverse side of the back board, measure from the base upward and mark a horizontal line at $\frac{3}{8}$ in. (15mm). From that mark, measure up $12\frac{3}{8}$ in. (315mm) and mark a second line, parallel to the first. Finally, measure up from the second line and mark a horizontal line $10\frac{1}{4}$ in. (260mm) from it. These lines give the position of the screw or nail holes that will attach the battens. Next, mark a second line, $\frac{1}{4}$ in. (6mm) below and parallel to each of the original lines, to show where the molding will be attached. To avoid confusion, use different colors for the markings or four pilot screw holes for each batten. Screw or nail the battens in place.

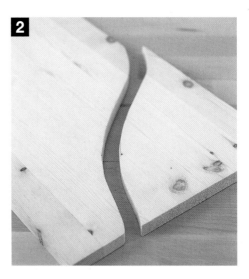

2 Using the template at the back of the book, trace the shaped curve onto the side pieces and cut them out with a jigsaw. Sand to finish and smooth the edges.

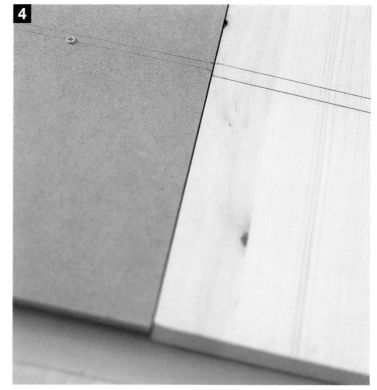

3 With sandpaper wrapped around a sanding block, chamfer the edges of the top piece.

4 Lay the two side pieces at either side of the back board and continue the bottom lines (the second set of lines you drew in the first step) across and onto each side. The bottom lines on all three pieces should align. As a guide, mark the thickness of the shelf on the side pieces.

5 To attach the sides to the back, apply glue and secure with miter clamps as shown—the back of the side pieces should be flush with the battens. Drill and screw through from the outside of the sides into the center of the battens.

6 Place the top on the sides, with an equal overhang at each end, and mark the positions. Remove and drill two pilot holes for each side through the top, then apply glue and screw in place.

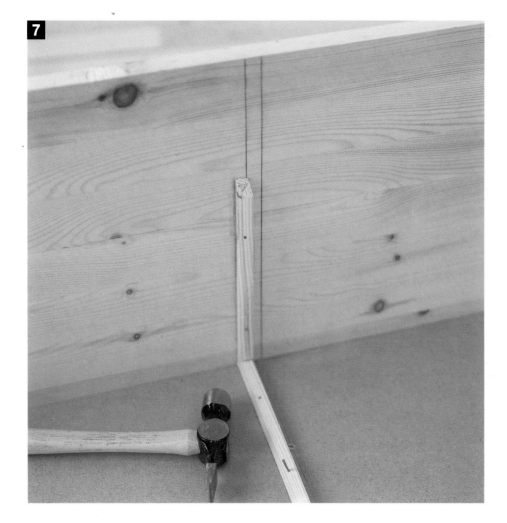

7 Cut and miter lengths of molding to support the shelves—it is important that you use flat-topped molding for the shelves to sit securely. Apply glue and nail the three long shelf supports to the back of the plate rack, using the pencil lines as a guide. Attach the six short side supports in the same way.

design tip

● This plate rack is a heavy item of furniture and must be secured safely to the wall. Fix two battens to the wall on which the top two shelf battens can sit, then screw through the shelf battens and into the wall. Use wall plugs for a secure fit.

9 Slot all three shelves into place. Finish by priming and painting the plate rack, then apply one or two coats of varnish for protection.

8 Glue and nail half a dowel to the front of the top two shelves—the shallower ones—to prevent plates stored there from slipping off.

you will need

- Pine shelf kit with solid-wood brackets
- Power drill
- Countersink and power-bore bits
- ⅜ or ½ in. (10 or 12mm) diameter dowel
- C-clamps
- Countersunk screws (optional)
- Screwdriver
- Tenon saw
- Sandpaper
- Wood glue
- Paint or woodstain and varnish

Customized shelf

Sometimes making a few additions or adjustments to an existing item can be very effective, and just as satisfying as making something from scratch. Adding a hanging rail to an easily available shelf kit instantly makes it twice as useful. The transformation takes a few minutes and is a great project for beginners.

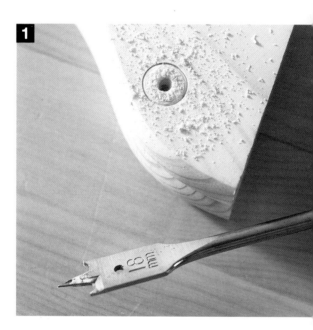

1 Work out the position of the holes through which the dowel will be threaded. You need to allow space behind them, so the holes should be on the wide part of the bracket. Mark the center of the holes. Clamp the brackets together to ensure that the holes align, then use a power-bore drill bit—which needs to be just larger than the diameter of the dowel—to drill a hole through both brackets.

2 Release the brackets from the clamps, then join the shelf and brackets together following the instructions supplied with the kit. If you feel that extra strength is needed, drill and countersink two screw holes through the top of the shelf into each bracket for extra strength.

3 Chamfer the ends of the dowel. Thread it through the holes in the brackets. If the dowel is a little loose, apply a little glue into the holes to keep it in place. Fill any screw holes in the top of the shelf, allow to dry, and sand.

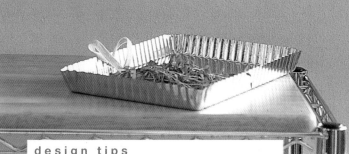

design tips

● The size of the dowel will depend on the size of the brackets. For large shelves and brackets, consider using larger diameter dowels.
● For a more contemporary look, replace the dowel with a chrome or metal pole. These are readily available at home improvement stores.

The Bedroom

Bedrooms may need to be everything from a home office to a playroom—as well somewhere to rest your head at night. A few key items of furniture that solve storage problems, screen off clutter, and create an elegant focal point, will ensure that your room is a tranquil haven where you can work, rest, or play.

Headboard

This headboard is simple and can be adapted for beds of all sizes. Give it a sun-bleached look with a pale wash that allows the grain of the wood to show through. A length of cord, threaded through the bed posts linking two decorative weights, provides a unique finishing touch.

you will need

- 12 pieces softwood 23⅝ x 2¾ x ¾ in. (600 x 70 x 19mm)
- 1 piece softwood 33¼ x 2¾ x ¾ in. (845 x 70 x 19mm)

Battens
- 2 pieces softwood 35⅜ x 2¾ x ¾ in. (900 x 70 x 19mm)

Posts
- 2 pieces softwood 52¾ x 1¾ x 1¾ in. (1340 x 45 x 45mm)
- Hammer
- Fine nails
- Power drill with ½ in. (12mm) flat bit and straight bit
- 1¾ in. (45mm) screws
- Diluted emulsion paint
- Cord
- 2 decorative weights
- Needle and coarse thread

1 Position the 12 planks face down on an even surface, butting them together along their length. Lay the two batten planks horizontally across them at top and bottom, with the edge of the battens 4 in. (100mm) from the top and base of the planks and overhanging equally on both sides. Hammer in fine nails at regular distances to secure the battens.

2 Mark a line 3 in. (75mm) from the top of each post, then use a power drill and ½ in. (12mm) flat bit to drill a hole through each post in the center of the line.

3 Position the posts along the sides of the planks, with the post tops 6 in. (150mm) beyond the plank tops. Drill pilot holes through the battens into the posts and drive in 1¾ in. (45mm) screws to secure.

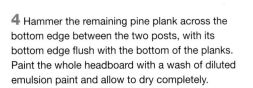

4 Hammer the remaining pine plank across the bottom edge between the two posts, with its bottom edge flush with the bottom of the planks. Paint the whole headboard with a wash of diluted emulsion paint and allow to dry completely.

design tip

● You can use anything decorative to weight the cord, as long as it is sufficiently heavy. Pebbles look lovely and are wonderful to the touch—perfect for a seaside bedroom. If you aren't lucky enough to find ones with ready-made holes, you could try making a spiral holding "cage" from strong wire. Wrap each pebble in wire, working it in a spiral, and loop the end through the cord.

5 Loop the cord through one weight and stitch it in place with coarse thread as shown. Thread the cord through the holes in each post and secure the second weight as before.

Storage box

This unique box can be put to many uses and makes a great low-level storage for anything from linens to shoes or magazines. If you prefer, you can make the box without the legs. For a dramatic finish, experiment with the wonderful metallic paints available in home improvement and paint stores.

you will need

Front and back
- 2 pieces MDF 37¼ x 12¼ x ½ in. (945 x 310mm x 12mm)

Sides
- 2 pieces MDF 12¼ x 10⅜ x ½ in. (310 x 264 x 12mm)

Base
- 1 piece MDF 36¼ x 10⅜ x ½ in. (920 x 264 x 12mm)

Lid
- 1 piece MDF 38 x 9¾ x ½ in. (965 x 250 x 12mm)
- 1 piece MDF 38 x 2½ x ½ in. (965 x 63 x 12mm)

Legs
- 2 pieces MDF 19⅝ x 15¾ x 1 in. (509 x 400 x 25mm)
- Miter clamps
- White glue
- Corner braces and screws
- Screwdriver
- ¼ in. (6mm) D-shaped molding
- Jigsaw
- Sandpaper and sanding block
- Pencil
- Hammer
- Brads
- Power drill and straight bit
- Nails
- 3 decorative hinges and screws
- Primer
- Silver paint and eggshell acrylic paint
- Decorative transfers (optional)

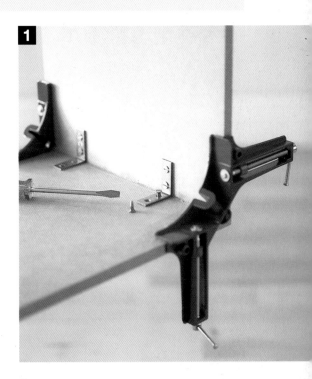

1 Attach one side piece to the front; lay the front down flat with a side piece perpendicular at one end. Apply glue along the edge of the side piece and place it on top, then secure with corner clamps before screwing in two corner braces. Repeat with the back and second side so that you end up with two L-shaped sections.

safety note

- Because the hinged lid is heavy and could slam shut on children's fingers, this item is not suitable for use in a child's room.

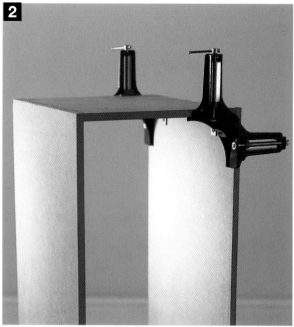

2 Join these two sections together so that you have a rectangular box. Apply glue and clamp, then screw in the corner braces as before.

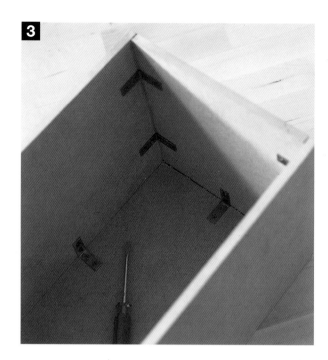

3 When fitting the rectangular box over the base piece, you cannot slot the base in from the top as the braces will get in the way. Instead, fix the box to the base using glue and two corner braces on each of the long sides, and one at each end.

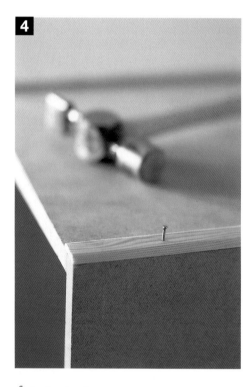

4 To disguise the joints at the ends of the box, cut D-shaped molding to length, then apply glue and fix it in position. Secure with brads, making sure that the pin heads are flush with the surface of the molding.

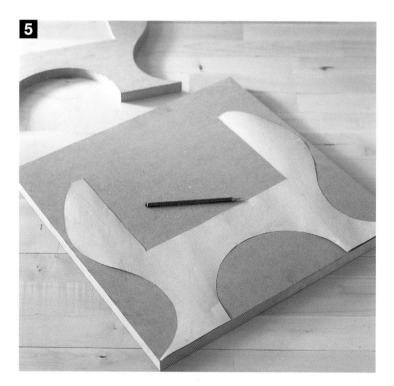

5 To make the legs, use a photocopier to enlarge the template at the back of the book to the required size. The legs should be 19⅝ in. (500mm) at the widest point, and the width of the gap should be fractionally larger than 11¾ in. (300mm) to allow for an easy fit. Trace the template twice onto a large sheet of MDF and cut out the legs with a jigsaw. Sand the edges to finish.

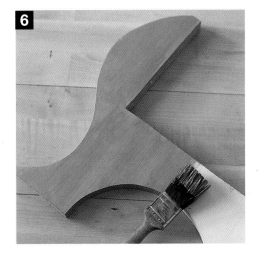

6 Prime both legs, not forgetting the edges. When the primer has dried thoroughly, apply one or two coats of silver-colored paint.

7 Prime and paint the box using acrylic eggshell paint. You should also paint both faces of the lid sections at this point, again remembering the edges.

design tips

● Look out for easy-to-use transfers that can transform a plain item of furniture almost instantly. For an understated look, use only a few or, if you prefer, you can decorate the box with stamps, stencils or small squares of metal leaf.

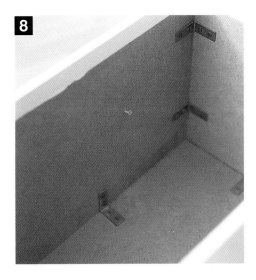

9 Join the two lid sections with decorative hinges at equal distances from the ends and in the middle.

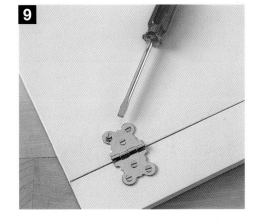

8 Stand the box on the legs, then mark and drill pilot holes through the base and sides. You will need two screws in the base and one at either side.

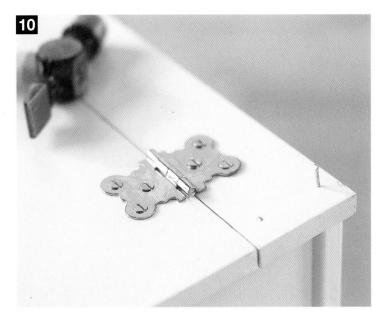

10 Apply glue to the thin lid section along its length and down each short side, then position it accurately on the box. To secure, hammer two nails in at either end and five along the back. Punch in and fill the heads, sand and touch up the paint.

Butler's tray

Based on a traditional design, this updated version of the classic butler's tray is an incredibly handy item and will come in useful time and time again. It can be used in virtually any room throughout the house, and is ideal for serving refreshments in the garden.

you will need

Frame
- 4 pieces stripwood 23⅝ x ¾ x ¾ in. (600 x 19 x 19mm)
- 2 dowels ⁵⁄₁₆ in. (8.5mm) and 14 in. (355mm)
- 2 dowels ⁵⁄₁₆ in. (8.5mm) and 12⅜ in. (315mm)
- 2 dowels ⁵⁄₁₆ in. (8.5mm) and 1½ in. (38mm)
- Power drill, ⁵⁄₁₆ in. (8.5mm) straight bit, and flat bit
- Masking tape
- White glue
- Fabric tape
- Staple gun

Tray base
- 1 piece MDF 19⅝ x 15¾ x ¼ in. (509 x 400 x 6mm)

Tray sides
- 2 pieces MDF 15⅜ x 3⅛ x ¼ in. (390 x 80 x 6mm)
- 2 pieces MDF 19¼ x 3⅛ x ¼ in. (490 x 80 x 6mm)
- Pencil
- Jigsaw
- Miter saw or back saw and miter block
- Sandpaper and sanding block
- Miter clamps
- Hammer
- Brads
- Primer and emulsion or acrylic paint
- Varnish (optional)
- 2 lengths cord

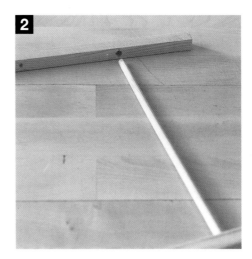

1 To make the frame, measure 4 in. (100mm) down from either end of the four pieces of stripwood, mark a line and then mark the center of the drill hole. Measure ⅜ in. (10mm) from the tip of the ⁵⁄₁₆ in. (8.5mm) drill bit and mark off the rest with masking tape. Drill halfway through each leg—to the edge of the tape on the bit—at the marked point. You should have eight holes in total.

2 Now you need to make two frames, each with two legs and two horizontal dowel bars. One is slightly narrower than the other, to allow it to slot inside the wider frame, so make sure that the two pieces of doweling for each frame are the same. Apply glue to the ends of the dowel and push them into the holes you have drilled.

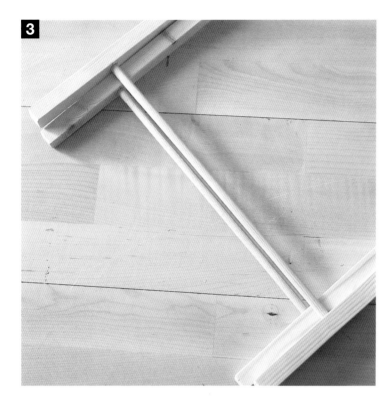

4 Mark the halfway point on each outside leg and find the center of the outside edge. Remove the tape from the bit and drill through each pair of legs from the outside in.

3 Slot the narrower frame through the wider one so that at one end a narrow dowel is on top and at the other end, underneath. This will enable the frames to pivot.

5 Use offcuts from the dowel to make two 1½ in. (38mm) long dowel pegs. Hammer these pegs through the holes on either side of each frame.

6 Paint the assembled frame. Open the frame so that the tray base can be placed on top with room to spare. Measure, cut, and staple two lengths of tape to link the top dowel bars to the two frames, then repeat for the bases.

7 On the tray base, measure in ³⁄₁₆in. (5mm) all around the four sides and mark in pencil to make guidelines for positioning the side pieces.

8 Use a miter saw or back saw and miter block to cut the four side pieces. Check that they will butt up neatly to one another when in place: sand to fit if required.

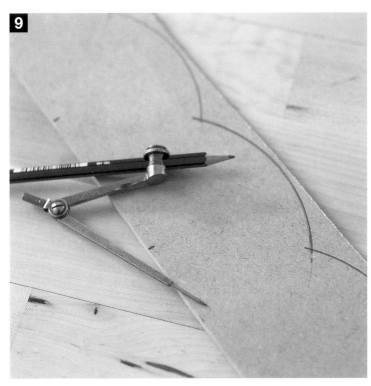

9 Use a compass or the template at the back of the book to mark the scalloped edges on the side pieces. Work out how many scallops you want and mark them in place. On the shorter pieces, a single scallop at either side linked by a larger, shallow shape is reasonably uncomplicated to cut out.

10 Clamp each side in turn and carefully cut out the scalloped edges with a jigsaw. Work a little at a time, starting at the top of each scallop and work down one side of the curve. It's easier to cut the same side of all the scallops before turning and reclamping the sides so that you can cut in the other direction.

11 Use a flat bit to drill holes for the handle cords below a depression of the scallop.

12 Apply glue to a long and short side, position and clamp with a corner clamp to secure, making sure that the mitered edges butt up neatly together. Repeat with the second pair of sides. When the glue has dried thoroughly, join the two L-shaped sections together to form the sides of the tray.

13 Apply glue to the tray's upper edge and place the base slightly protruding on all sides. Hammer in brads at regular distances, using the pencil lines as a guide. Prime and paint the tray, allow to dry; varnish the tray and frame. When dry, loop cord through the drilled holes and knot the ends.

Children's Rooms

A child's room is full of design possibilities—and the good news is that the simplest ideas are often the best. Put your new skills to work and brighten up existing furniture, or even create exciting new projects.

Starfish mirror

This fun frame looks great in bedrooms or bathrooms, and could be adapted for all sorts of uses. You might like to take the underwater theme further and use the template as a basis for a multicolored mural.

you will need

- 1 piece ¼ in. (6mm) thick MDF
- Pencil
- Circular mirror
- Power drill and straight bit
- Jigsaw
- Sandpaper and sanding block
- Stipple brush
- Emulsion paint
- Bubble wrap
- Small paintbrush
- 2 pieces ¾ x ¾ in. (19 x 19mm) hardboard
- Epoxy resin adhesive
- Small brads
- Hammer
- Hanging hooks
- Picture wire

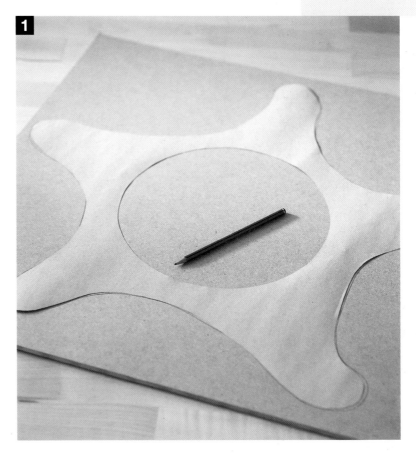

1 On a photocopier, blow up the template at the back of the book to the size that you require, using your mirror as a guide to scale. With a pencil, draw around the paper template onto the MDF, then draw a circle in the center for the mirror. The diameter of the circular hole should be around ⅜–¾ in. (10–19 mm) smaller than the actual mirror.

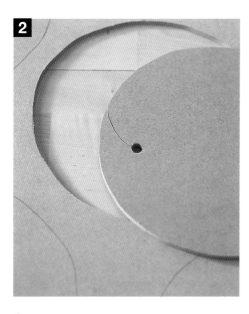

2 To cut out the circular center of the frame, drill a small hole inside the inner circle and use a jigsaw to cut out the circle counterclockwise (clockwise if you are left-handed). Next, use the jigsaw to cut around the outer edge of the starfish frame. Lightly sand the edges to finish.

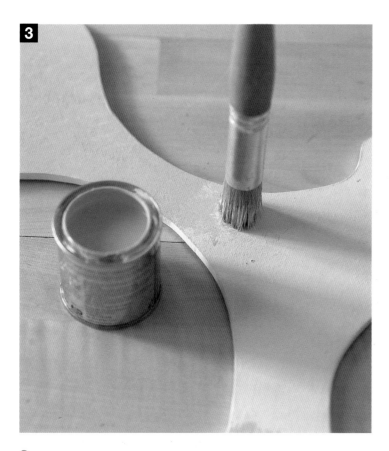

3 Paint the frame using a stippling brush to give a slightly textured effect. Don't forget to paint the side edges of the MDF too. Allow to dry completely.

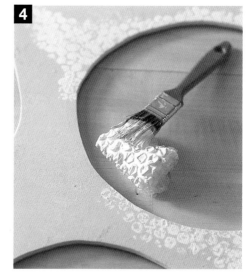

4 Fold over a small piece of bubble wrap, with the bubbles on the outside, and coat the surface lightly with a small paintbrush—do not dip the bubblewrap into a tray of paint, as this will ruin the result. Press the painted surface down firmly all around the circular rim to make a narrow band of pattern. Then use the same technique to make a tapered band down the center of each arm.

5 When the paint has dried, turn the mirror over. On the reverse glue down two small squares of hardboard, at an equal distance on either side of the frame. This is used to screw in hanging hooks at the end.

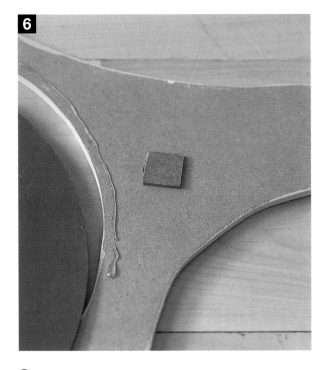

6 Glue the mirror to the back of the frame using epoxy resin adhesive, following the instructions on the package.

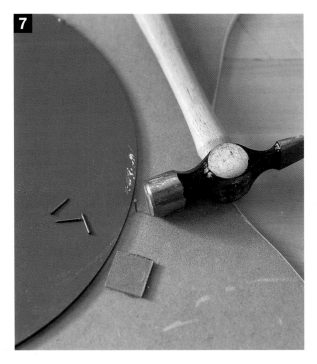

7 To make the mirror more secure, hammer in small brads around the edge, starting straight and then knocking them in at an angle toward the mirror to anchor it. Screw the hanging hooks into the hardboard squares, making sure that they do not protrude through the front of the frame. Thread picture wire between the hanging hooks, and the mirror is ready to hang on the wall.

Beach hut screen

Children's rooms could always do with more space—but as it is difficult to create more room in a limited space, why not do the next best thing, and hide everything that doesn't need to be on display behind a neat little screen? This simple design, painted to look like a row of summer beach huts, is perfect for disguising clutter—and can even double as a little playhouse or theater.

you will need

- Three pieces 48 x 24 x ¹/₂ in (1220 x 610 x 12mm) MDF or wood
- Jigsaw
- Sandpaper and block
- Wood glue
- Power drill
- Screwdriver
- Fine nails
- Center punch
- Bradawl
- Four 16in (405mm) lengths of ³⁄₈in. (10mm) quarter-profile molding
- Four 2½in (63mm) screen hinges
- Masking tape
- Wood filler
- Emulsion paints
- Clear varnish
- Pair of compasses

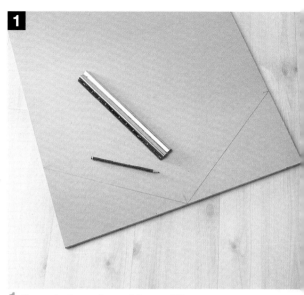

1 To create the roofs, mark in pencil the midpoint, 12 in. (305mm), on the shorter edge of each piece of MDF or softwood—this is the apex. Now measure 8 in. (200mm) down on each of the long sides and mark carefully. Ensure that your measuring is accurate, or you may end up with skewed roofs. Using a steel rule and pencil, draw a line to link each of the side marks with the central mark at the top of each piece.

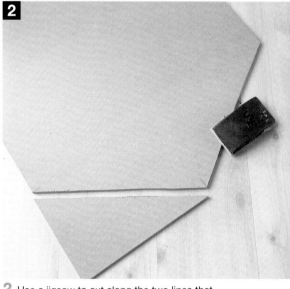

2 Use a jigsaw to cut along the two lines that you have drawn, to form a pointed shape. Do this on each of the three pieces. When you have completed this, use sandpaper, wrapped around a wood or cork sanding block, to sand along the newly cut rough edges and give a smooth finish.

3 Measure and mark 32 in. (815mm) up from the base on each side, then join the lines across. This is the top edge of the window frame. For the bottom edge, mark up 16 in. (405mm) from the base on each side, then join the marks. For the frame sides, measure and mark 4 in. (100mm) in along the two lines from each side. Drill a hole at each corner to help you cut cleanly. With a jigsaw, cut out the window, moving from corner to corner.

4 To finish off the window, you need to apply quarter-profile molding. Cut four 16 in. (405mm) lengths to fit along the sides of the cut-out square. Glue all the pieces in place, and when the glue has dried, hammer in fine nails along the inner edges of the frame at 4 in. (100m) intervals. Use a center punch and hammer to gently tap the nail heads just below the surface of the wood, then fill the holes with a little wood filler and allow to dry completely before gently sanding the filler flush.

5 Prime the front, back, and edges of all three pieces of the screen with white emulsion. When the paint has dried completely, measure along the base of each section and mark out the positions of the colored stripes. The stripes pictured here are around 4 in. (100mm) wide. Draw the stripes in pencil, using a steel ruler for accuracy. To get a really crisp border for the stripes, firmly apply masking tape along the pencil lines.

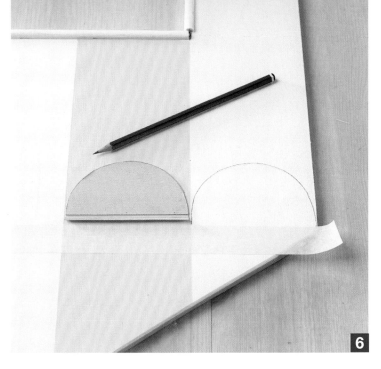

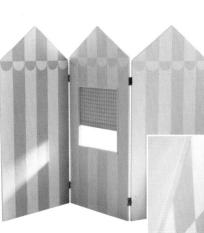

6 Lightly draw a horizontal line across the base of each roof, and apply masking tape above the line. For the scalloped decoration, set a pair of compasses to a diameter fractionally smaller than the width of the stripes. Draw the circle on a piece of cardboard and cut in half. Place the straight edge of the template on the guide line and trace the outline of the shape onto each stripe. Paint the scallops in alternate colors. Allow to almost dry, then remove the tape as before and let dry. Erase the guide line and sand the surfaces.

design tips

● To finish the screen, apply layers of clear acrylic varnish when the paint has dried, and fit curtains or a blind above the window.
● You can choose stripes of any width, but remember that a narrow design will be trickier to paint.
● In a room that is used by small children, attach one end to the wall with a hook to avoid the screen overbalancing.
● Experiment with different paint effects to create a puppet theater

7 Paint on the contrasting stripes with colored emulsion, making sure that you cover the surface well—you may need to apply a second coat. At the edges, brush on the paint so that it goes right up to the border and just onto the masking tape—don't flood the edge, or the paint will creep under the tape. Leave the paint until it is almost dry before carefully removing the tape, then touch-up any rough edges and allow to dry completely.

8 Lay the central section flat. For the bottom of the lower hinge, mark 6 in. (150mm) up from the base on each side; for the top of the upper hinge, mark 6 in. (150mm) down from the top of the scallops. Position the hinges and mark screw holes, leaving the other hole. Mark the screw centers, then insert the screws. Lay one side piece next to the central one, making sure that the bases align. Open the hinges and mark screw holes on the side piece. The edge of the hinge plate should be flush with the edge of the side piece, with the hinge barrel overhanging slightly. Repeat on the other side.

design tips

● This is an excellent way of using up small amounts of emulsion paint that have been leftover after decorating a child's room, or any of the painted projects in this book.

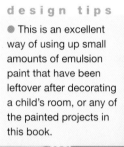

Decorative Shelves

Plain self-assembly shelving units are relatively inexpensive—however, though they are undoubtedly useful, they can look bland. So why not give them a quick makeover? These projects can be finished in a day, and are ideal for beginners to woodwork—children can help to paint it.

you will need

- ¼ in. (6mm) thick MDF
- Pencil
- Back saw
- Sandpaper and sanding block
- Primer
- Emulsion paints
- Matte varnish
- Upholstery tacks
- Hammer
- Pliers
- Epoxy resin adhesive
- Artist's brush

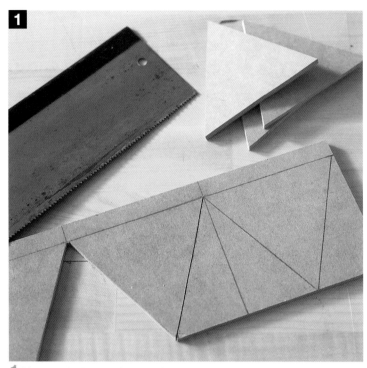

1 Measure the length of the shelf you want to decorate. Trace the shape onto a piece of MDF. Use a back saw to cut out the pointed shape. You will find it easiest to start at the bottom point of each triangle and work inward, cutting first along one of its sides and then the other.

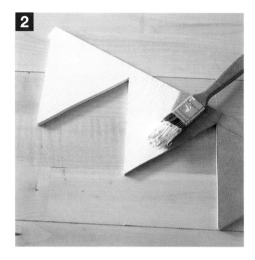

2 Lightly sand the cut edges to finish, brush the dust off, and prime.

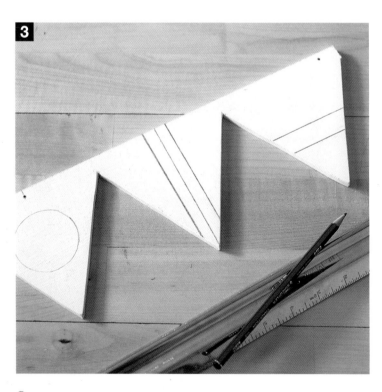

3 Using a pencil, outline the designs that you want to make on each flag. For the best effect, mix a variety of simple designs in a random arrangement.

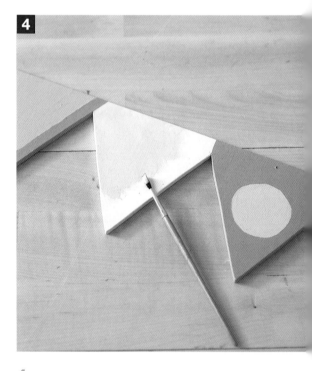

4 With an artist's brush, fill in the shapes on the primed shapes in three or four shades of paint that will complement your color scheme. When the paint is completely dry, apply a couple of coats of matte varnish for extra protection.

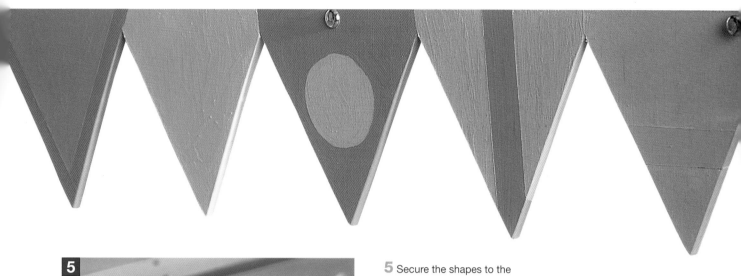

5 Secure the shapes to the shelving unit with upholstery tacks. Before hammering them in, make three small pilot holes in each piece of MDF. Cover the hammer head with a scrap piece of fabric to protect the upholstery tack heads.

6 To finish off the piece, decorate the shelving unit itself with some of the remaining tacks. Cut the pointed ends off with pliers and then glue the upholstery tacks to the frame with a strong adhesive such as epoxy resin.

The Bathroom

A small bathroom can look cluttered when filled with different styles of furniture and accessories, so we made these items all in one style for a clean, unified look. The slatted mat, featured in all three projects, is simple to make using spacers. A simple paint finish is modern and fresh and adds to style.

Slatted mat

On a tiled or vinyl floor, a slatted wooden bath mat is not only stylish and elegant, but is also more sanitary than an old-fashioned cloth mat. If you want to make a longer one, you may need to add another crosspiece to prevent the slats from bending.

you will need

CROSSPIECES
- 3 pieces softwood 16¼ x ⅞ x ⅞ in. (410 x 22 x 22mm)

SLATS
- 8 pieces softwood 24 x ⅞ x ⅞ in. (610 x 22 x 22mm)

SPACER
- 1 piece MDF 24 x 1⅜ x ½ in. (620 x 35 x 13mm)
- 24 galvanized woodscrews 1⅜ x ⅛ in (35 x 4mm)
- Pencil
- Try square
- Power drill and ⅛ in. (4mm) straight bit
- Sandpaper and sanding block
- Screwdriver
- Emulsion paint and rag
- Polyurethane varnish
- Paintbrush

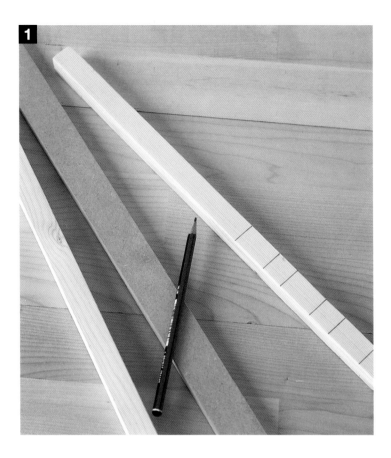

1 On one of the crosspieces, mark off divisions with the spacer and one of the slats. Lay the slat across the crosspiece, flush with the end, and draw a pencil line. Remove the slat, lay the spacer against the pencil line and draw another line. Continue marking alternate slat and spacer divisions right down the crosspiece, ending with a slat, which should be flush with the end. Align the other two crosspieces with the marked one and, using a try square, continue the pencil lines across all the crosspieces.

2 Fit a ⅛ in. (4mm) straight bit into a power drill and drill a hole through the center of each slat space on all three crosspieces. To find the true center, draw diagonal lines between the corners of the slat spaces.

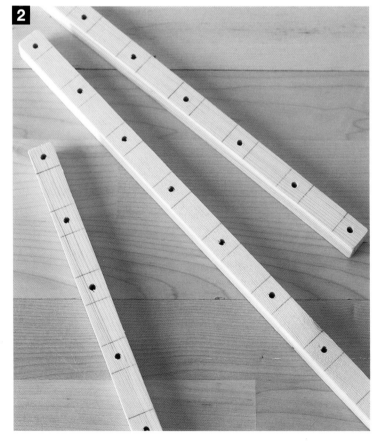

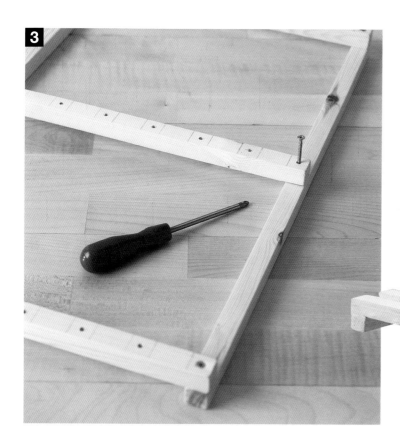

● A matching soap dish is simple to make: simply use two crosspieces and five slats, and reduce all the dimensions, including the screws; assemble in the same way.

● Experiment with two washes of different colors on a piece of scrap wood—if you like the effect, use it on the finished mat.

3 Lay one of the slats on a flat surface and position the crosspieces at right angles on top of it, the ends of the crosspieces flush with the side of the slat. To keep the crosspieces level, put another slat under the far end. One crosspiece should lie exactly across the middle of the slat, and the others should align with each end. Use a bradawl to mark down through the predrilled hole in each cross piece of the slat. Screw the two end pieces first, then the middle one.

4 Lay the spacer under the crosspieces, flush against one end slat. Push the next slat up against the spacer, then bradawl and screw down through the holes as before. Continue in this way until all the slats are attached to the crosspieces. For a limewashed look, wipe the surface with a rag soaked in diluted white emulsion paint. When dry, seal with two coats of polyurethane varnish.

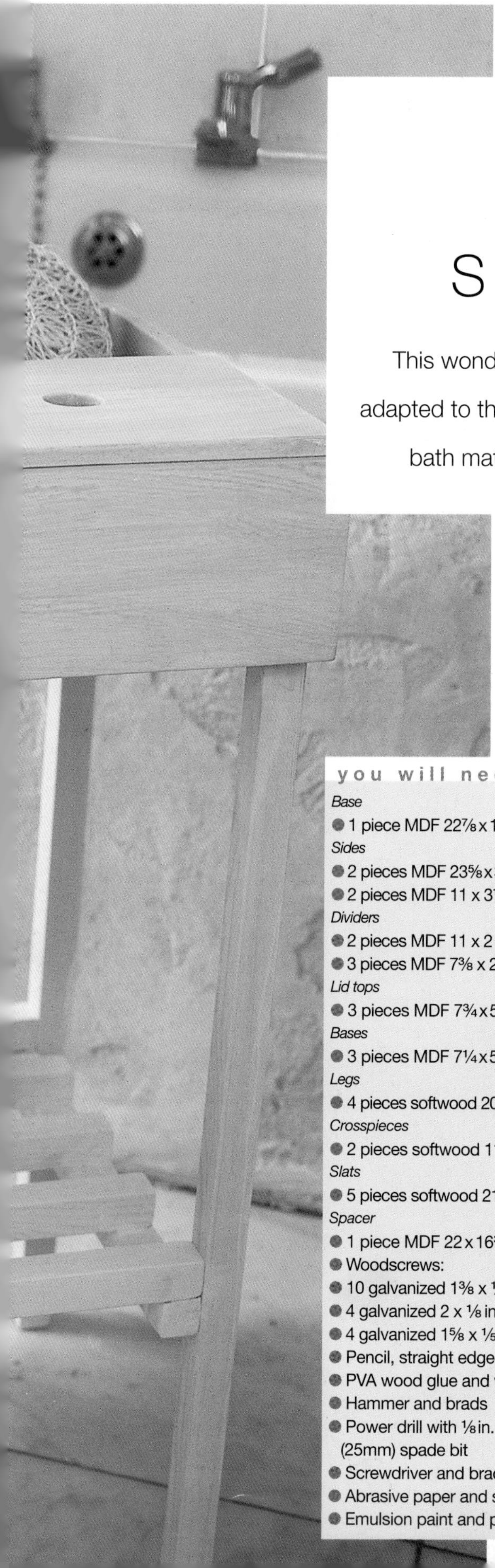

Bathroom storage unit

This wonderfully useful unit is based on the traditional butler's tray, but adapted to the needs of the modern bathroom. The shelf is the basic slatted bath mat, while the top provides clever storage space for toiletries.

1 Measure up ⅞in. (22mm) from the bottom of both long and both short sides, and use a straight edge to draw a line between the marks.

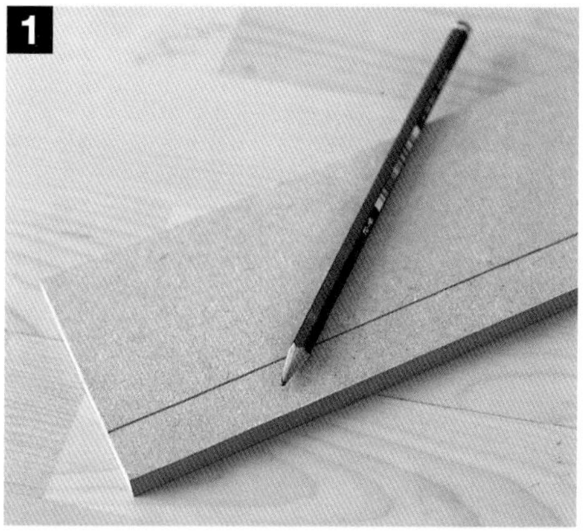

you will need

Base
- 1 piece MDF 22⅞ x 11 x ¾in. (582 x 280 x 18mm)

Sides
- 2 pieces MDF 23⅝ x 3½ x ⅜in (600 x 88 x 10mm)
- 2 pieces MDF 11 x 3½ x ⅜ in. (280 x 88 x 10mm)

Dividers
- 2 pieces MDF 11 x 2 x ⅜ in. (280 x 50 x 10mm)
- 3 pieces MDF 7⅜ x 2 x ⅜ in. (188 x 50 x 10mm)

Lid tops
- 3 pieces MDF 7¾ x 5¾ x ⅜in. (195 x 145 x 10mm)

Bases
- 3 pieces MDF 7¼ x 5¼ x ⅜in. (185 x 135 x 10mm)

Legs
- 4 pieces softwood 20⅞ x ⅞ x ⅞in. (532 x 22 x 22mm)

Crosspieces
- 2 pieces softwood 11 x ⅞ x ⅞in. (280 x 22 x 22mm)

Slats
- 5 pieces softwood 21¼ x ⅞ x ⅞in. (540 x 22 x 22mm)

Spacer
- 1 piece MDF 22 x 16¾ x ⅜in. (560 x 425 x 10mm)
- Woodscrews:
- 10 galvanized 1⅜ x ⅛ in. (35 x 4mm)
- 4 galvanized 2 x ⅛ in. (50 x 4mm)
- 4 galvanized 1⅝ x ⅕ in. (40 x 4mm)
- Pencil, straight edge, and try square
- PVA wood glue and wood filler
- Hammer and brads
- Power drill with ⅛in. (4mm) straight bit and 1 in. (25mm) spade bit
- Screwdriver and bradawl
- Abrasive paper and sanding block
- Emulsion paint and polyurethane varnish

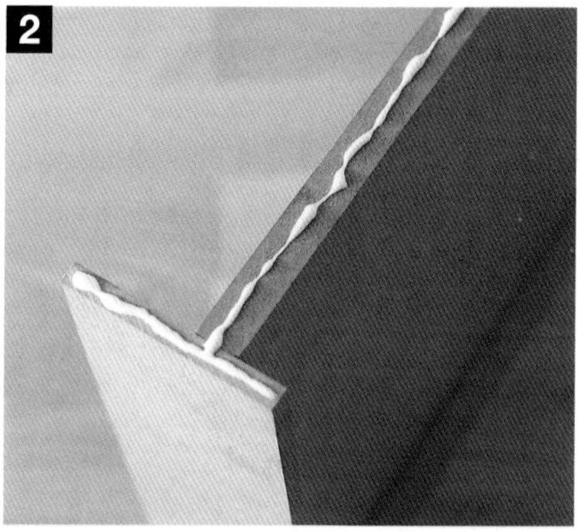

2 One side at a time, run a line of glue along an edge of the base, and lay a side piece against it with the pencil line level with the bottom of the base. Do the short sides first, then the long sides to make a tray.

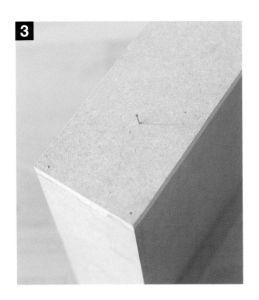

3 Make sure that the base and sides meet at right angles, then hammer brads through each side at a time into the edge of the base, spacing them at roughly 3 in. (75mm) intervals. Allow the glue to dry.

4 Measure and draw a line lengthwise down the middle of the tray. Use two of the short dividers as spacers to set the position of the first long divider across the tray. Position the spacers as shown, put in the long divider, and draw a pencil line down each side of it. Remove the long divider, leaving the short dividers in place.

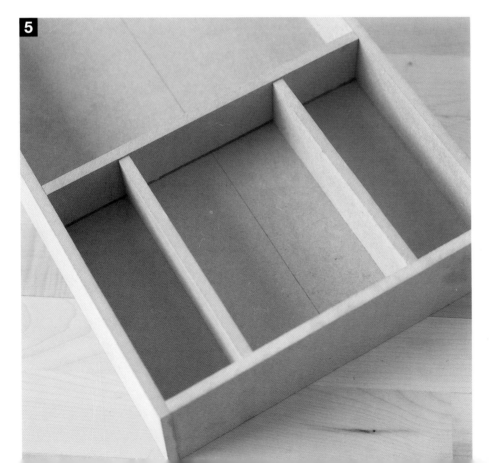

5 Run a line of wood glue along the bottom and side edges of a long divider and stand it between the pencil lines in front of the short dividers. Check for right angles and leave to dry. Remove the short dividers and, working from the other end of the tray, use them to position the second long divider in the same way.

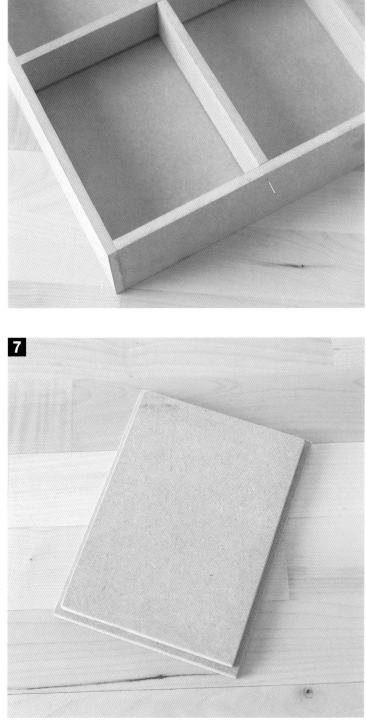

6 One section at a time, run a line of wood glue along the bottom and side edges of a short divider and stand it on the pencil line, then leave to dry. Hammer two brads through the sides of the tray into the end of each of the four dividers. Mark a hole ½ in. (12mm) from each corner of the top of the base, then use a straight bit to drill through the hole.

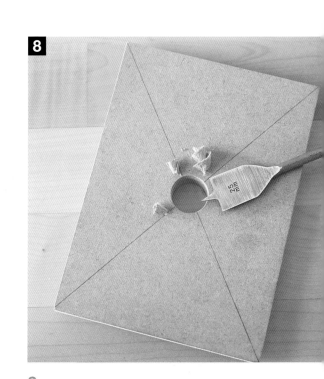

8 Find the center of each lid top by drawing two diagonal lines between the corners—the point where they meet is the center. Drill a hole right through the center of the lids with a power drill using a 1 in. (25mm) spade drill bit.

7 Position the lid bases so they are central, then mark around the bases with a pencil. Remove the bases, apply glue to them, and fix them firmly into position. Allow to dry.

9 Make a slatted shelf in the same way as the slatted mat on page 98, but with only two crosspieces, one at each end.

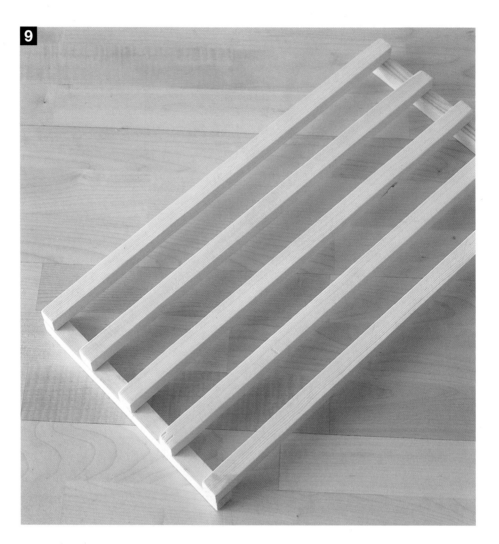

10 Mark a hole 8 in. (200mm) up from the bottom of each leg, then use a straight bit to drill through the legs. Position Working one leg at a time, apply glue to the top and to the top ¾ in. (19mm) of two sides. Position the leg in a corner of the underside of the tray, with the glued sides against the edges of the tray and the predrilled hole facing the center of the tray. Rest the other end of the leg on the shelf spacer to hold it level.

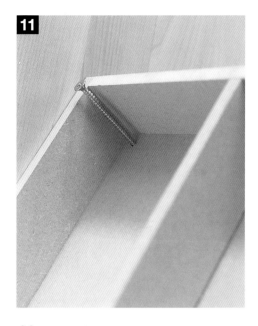

11 Screw down through the hole in the top of the tray into the top of the leg. Attach the other legs in the same way.

12 Position the slatted shelf between the legs, level with the predrilled holes, bradawl through into the shelf, and screw through the legs into the end grain of the slats.

13 Fill and sand all panel holes. Prime the tray and lids, then paint the inside of the tray with emulsion. Decorate the outside of the tray and the tops of the lids by soaking a rag with diluted emulsion paint and wiping it over the surface. Decorate the legs and slatted tray with diluted white emulsion in the same way to give a limewashed look. Seal the whole unit with two coats of polyurethane varnish.

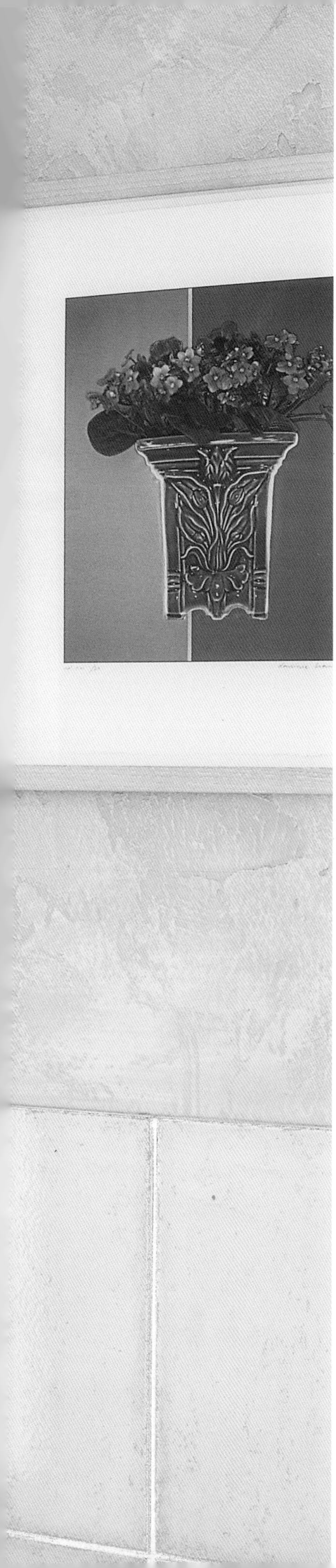

Peg rail

Places to put flannels, towels, and other bath-time accessories are always welcome, even in large bathrooms. This peg rail solves the storage problem with minimal fuss and completes the matching set, giving your bathroom a touch of class.

you will need

- **CROSSPIECES** ● 2 pieces softwood $11\frac{3}{8}$ x $\frac{7}{8}$ x $\frac{7}{8}$in. (290 x 22 x 22mm)
- **SLATS** ● 6 pieces softwood $23\frac{5}{8}$ x $\frac{7}{8}$ x $\frac{7}{8}$in. (600 x 22 x 22mm)
- **SPACER** ● 1 piece MDF 24 x $1\frac{3}{5}$ x $\frac{1}{2}$in. (620 x 35 x 12mm)
- **RAIL BACK BOARD** ● 1 piece softwood $23\frac{5}{8}$ x $5\frac{3}{4}$ x $\frac{3}{4}$in. (600 x 145 x 19mm)
- **PEGS** ● 4 wooden dowels $4\frac{3}{4}$in. (120mm) long and 1 in. (25mm) diameter
- **BRACKETS** ● 2 pieces softwood $4\frac{3}{8}$ x $4\frac{3}{8}$ x $\frac{3}{4}$in. (110 x 110 x 19mm)
- **BACK BARS** ● 2 pieces softwood 13 x $1\frac{3}{4}$ x $\frac{3}{4}$in. (330 x 45 x 19mm)
- 8 galvanized woodscrews $1\frac{3}{8}$ x $\frac{1}{8}$in. (35 x 4mm)
- Pencil
- Straight edge
- Try square
- Power drill with $\frac{1}{8}$in. (4mm) straight bit and 1 in. (25mm) spade bit
- Screwdriver and bradawl
- Abrasive paper and sanding block
- Wood glue and wood filler
- Emulsion paint
- Polyurethane varnish

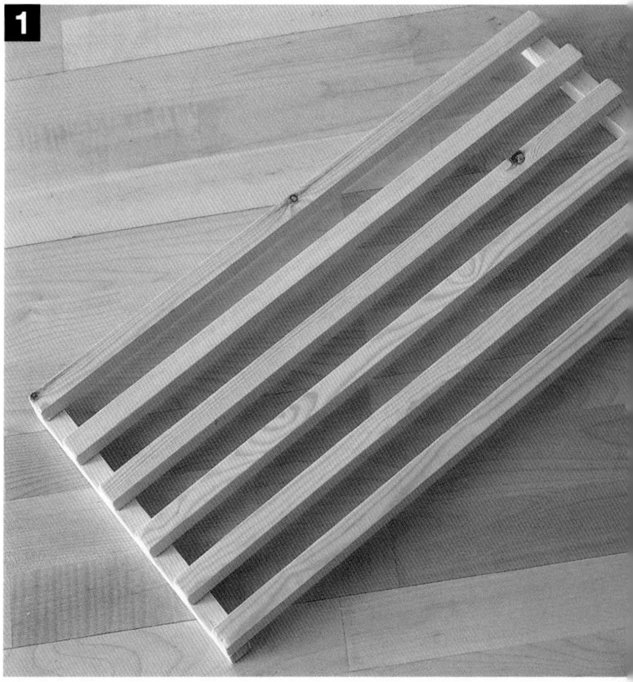

1 Make up a slatted shelf in the same way as the slatted mat on page 98, this time using only two crosspieces, one at each end.

2

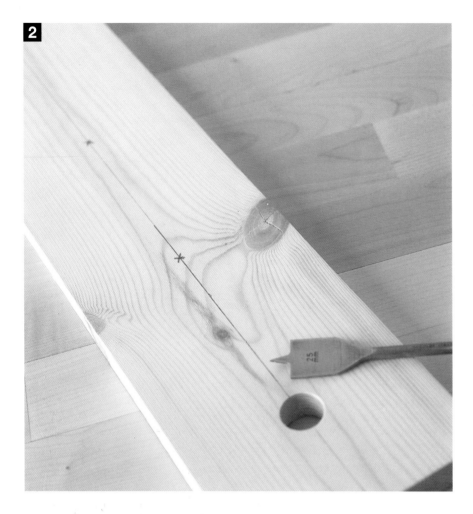

2 Draw a pencil line lengthwise across the middle of the rail back board. Make a pencil mark on this line 3 in. (75mm) in from each end and then two more marks 6 in. (150mm) in from the first two. Drill a hole at each marked point with a 1 in. (25mm) spade bit.

3

3 Chamfer the ends of each piece of dowel.

4

4 Apply white glue around the end of each piece of dowel and push it to fit firmly into the drilled holes in the back board. Check that the pegs are at right angles to the board and leave to dry.

5

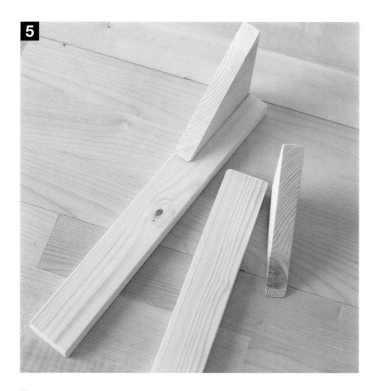

6

5 Cut two brackets to size and then place one against each back bar, flush with the top and aligned against opposite sides. Mark the position and use the ⅛ in. (4mm) straight bit to drill two pilot holes from the back of each bar into the bracket. Insert the screws and tighten them.

6 Mark ⅞ in. (22mm) in from each ends of the back board. Use the ⅛ in. (4mm) straight bit to drill two pilot holes from the back of each bar into the board. Screw into position.

7 Position the shelf on the brackets, with the top of each bracket flush with the inside of the crosspieces. Drill two pilot holes through each brackets into the crosspieces and screw in place—check first that the screws will not hit the screws holding the slats to the crosspieces. Fill all screw holes with wood filler and sand flush when dry.

7

The Garden

Whether you are an avid gardener or simply view your garden as an extra, outdoor room, you can add to your enjoyment of being outdoors with these simple projects, that have a distinctly designer look—but which cost considerably less to make than mass-produced, store-bought items.

Garden bench

Make the most of summer weather with this stylish garden bench. It's simple to put together, so after you've got the hang of how to make it, experiment with different sizes and colors to create a versatile range of outdoor furniture that will grace any garden.

you will need

Top
- 1 piece pine
  48 x 10½ x 1in.
  (1220 x 267 x 25mm)

Sides
- 2 pieces pine
  48 x 10 x 1 in.
  (1220 x 255 x 25mm)

Legs
- 2 pieces pine
  14 x 10¼ x 1in.
  (355 x 260 x 25mm)
- Galvanized screws and nails
- Jigsaw and pencil
- Drill and straight bit
- Sandpaper and sanding block
- Miter clamps
- Wood filler
- Exterior wood stain

1 To make the notches in each leg, measure along the base—the 10½ in. (267mm) edge—of each leg to find the midpoint, mark it, then divide the section on either side in two so that the leg is divided into four. Now measure around 4¾ in. (120mm) up from the midpoint and mark. At this point, drill a hole to form the apex of the cutout notch. Find the quarter sections marked on the base and cut out the triangular section with a jigsaw. Each time, start at the base and work toward the drilled hole. Sand the newly cut surfaces thoroughly.

2 Now you need to attach the legs to the top of the bench. Around 4¾ in. (120mm) in from each end of the top, mark a line on the underside. These lines should be parallel to the ends and to each other. Glue and clamp the legs in place. For extra security, when the glue has dried, turn the bench over and drill three holes through the seat into each leg and punch in 2 in. (50mm) galvanized nails. Fill the holes with wood filler and sand down when dry.

3 To attach the two sides, first angle the corners with a jigsaw. To ensure a neat finish, place each side against the bench and mark the thickness of the top section on the outer edges . After cutting, sand thoroughly. Countersink five holes along each side section. The two outer holes should be around 3 in. (75mm) in from the sides. Screw each side onto the bench, then drill two additional holes over each leg section and screw in place.

4 If your bench is for outdoor use, finish it with a wood stain or paint recommended for garden furniture—and don't forget to coat the underside of the legs. For indoor use, you can get away with a coat or two of emulsion. Either way, give the bench a weathered look by lightly sanding the outer edges between coats.

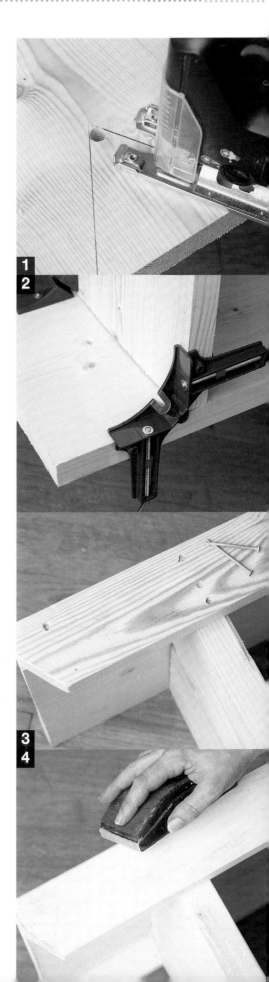

Planter Covers

Plastic troughs are an inexpensive way of displaying colorful flowers and foliage, but they don't look very inspiring. These simple, wooden slip-over covers transform plastic planters in an instant and can be switched around to coordinate with different plants and colors. The sizes given here are to match standard plastic troughs.

you will need

Front and back
- 2 pieces softwood 36⅝ x 25⅝ x ½ in. (930 x 650 x 12mm)

Sides
- 2 pieces softwood 23⅝ x 25⅝ x ½ in. (600 x 650 x 12mm)
- Jigsaw
- Pencil
- Tracing paper
- Sandpaper and sanding block
- Miter clamps
- 8 corrugated fastenings
- Hammer
- Colored exterior woodstain

1 Choose a template design from the ones at the back of the book. Increase the dimensions for your cover using a photocopier. Cut out the template and draw around it to transfer the design onto the front and back pieces of your cover. Cut the pieces out carefully with a jigsaw, and sand to finish the edges.

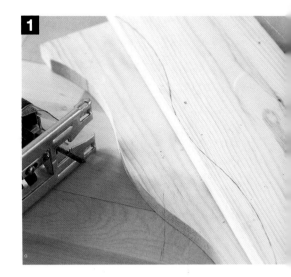

2 Clamp the front and sides together using a couple of corner clamps. You should inset the sides very slightly—around ⅜ in. (10mm) or so is ideal.

design tips

● Adapt the design to suit the size of your planter—or why not come up with a template of your own?

● Because these covers have no base, you don't have to worry about drainage. They simply slot over the top of plastic troughs to give the appearance of a wooden window box or planter.

3 Hammer in corrugated fastenings at a diagonal across the top and bottom of each join to secure. Attach the back piece in the same way and finish off with a colored woodstain, specially formulated for outdoor use.

Bamboo planter

This planter is extremely inexpensive to make—and doesn't require much in the way of special tools or materials. You will need to be patient, however, as some of the steps are a bit cumbersome. Take your time, and you'll be rewarded with a handsome-looking garden container that's a true original.

you will need

- Stripwood ⅝ x ⅝ in. (22 x 22mm)
- Saw or jigsaw
- Miter clamps
- ⅛ in. (3.5mm) brads
- Glue gun and glue sticks
- Bamboo

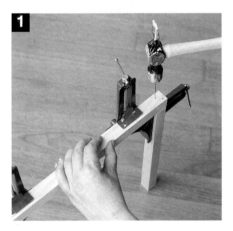

1 To make the basic frame of the planter, you will need to make one square to form the top and another for the base. These are each made from two 14 in. (355mm) pieces and two 10¼ in. (260mm) pieces. With this method there's no need for mitered corners. Glue and clamp the wood to form the frames, and secure with brads as shown. Leave to dry thoroughly.

2 Now join the top and bottom by attaching the four leg sections to create a "box." The top of each leg should come halfway up the inside of the upper frame. Use wood glue and brads to secure as before. Fit the bottom frame over the legs after the top section is in place.

3 Next you need to attach the slats to the base of the planter. Place the frame top down and butt a slat up to each pair of legs, then space the remaining slats around ⅜ in. (16mm) apart. Attach each one with wood glue and a brad at each end.

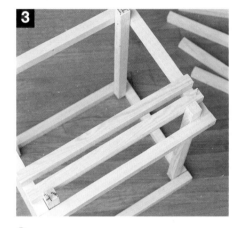

4 Now you're ready to attach the bamboo. Before you start, cut plenty of lengths to size—you'll be surprised at how much you use. Clean the bamboo thoroughly by wiping with mineral spirits to ensure that the glue adheres properly. Now attach each stick of bamboo, top and bottom, with a dab of hot glue from a glue gun. If you haven't got a glue gun, you can use ordinary wood glue—but be prepared to wait a little longer for the glue to dry.

p28 Letter rack

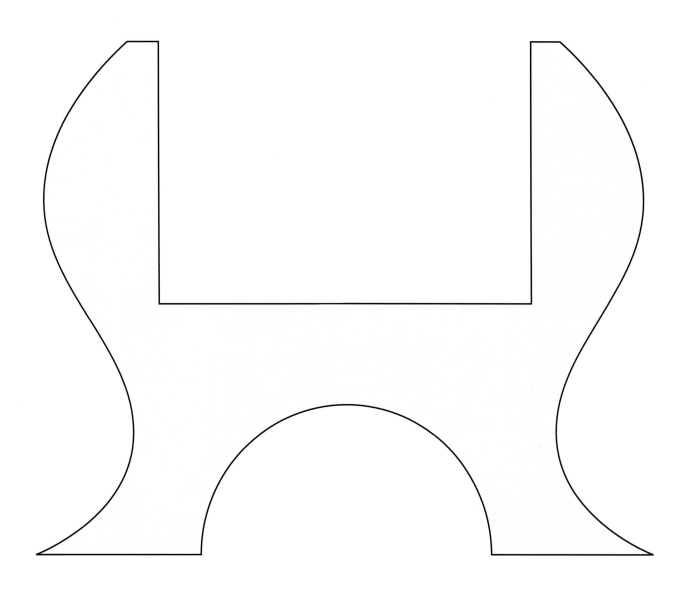

p72 Storage box

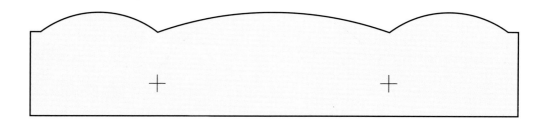

p76 Butler's tray

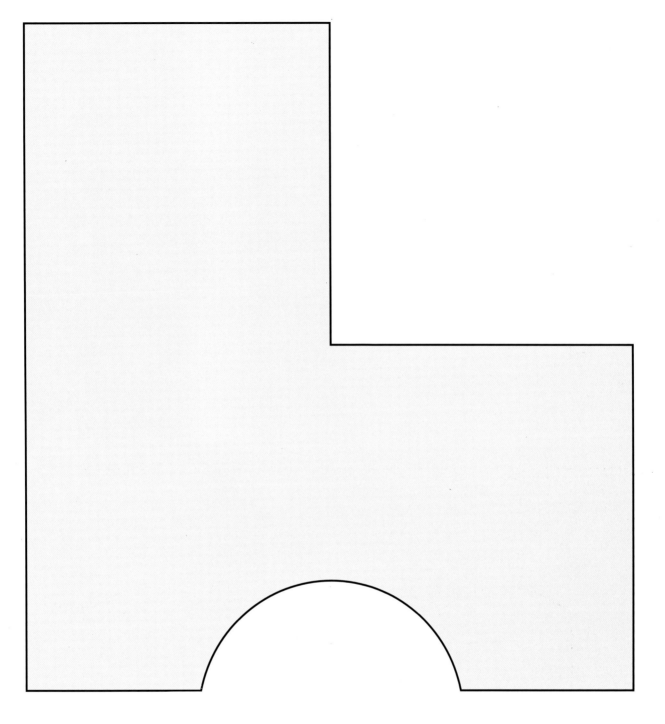

p54 Step stool

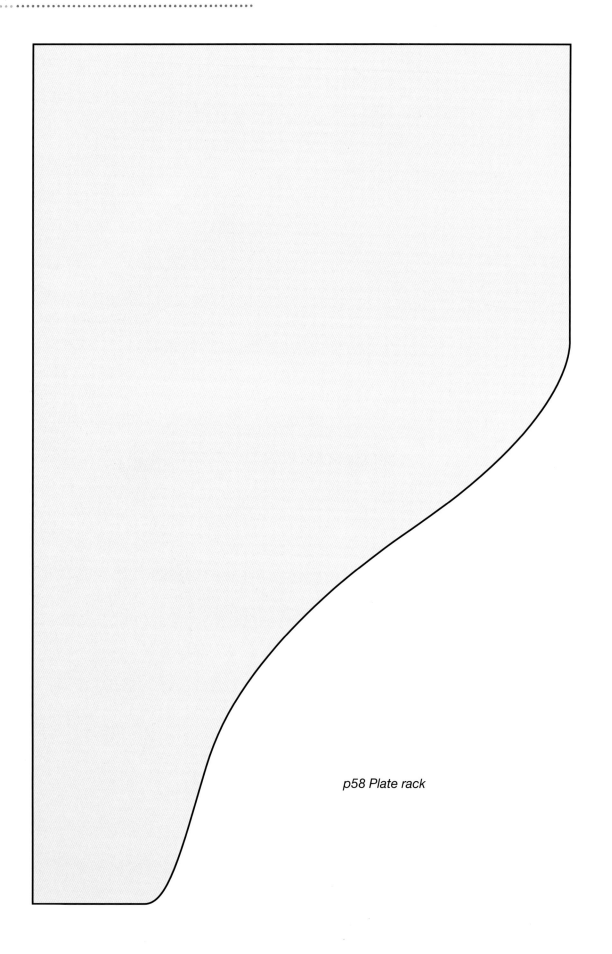

p58 Plate rack

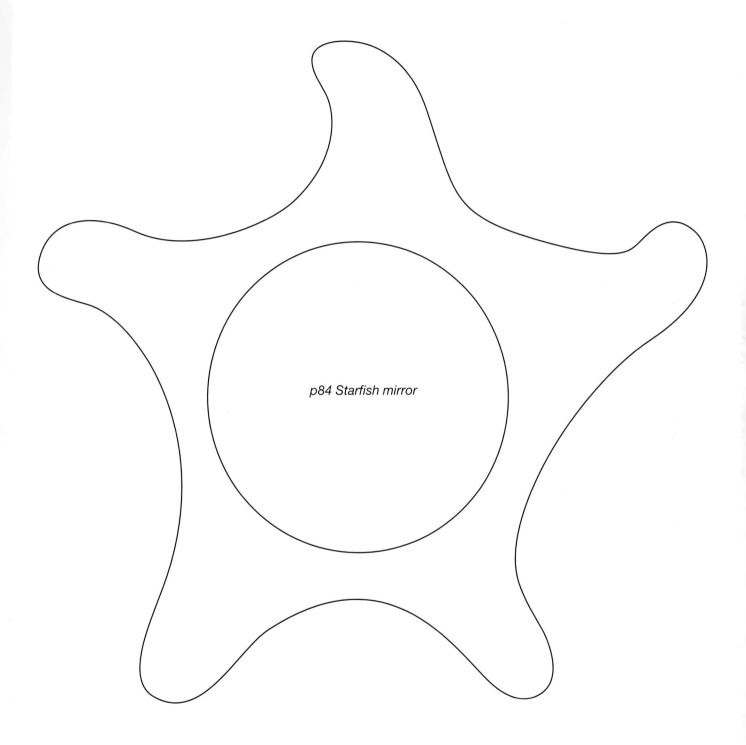

p84 Starfish mirror

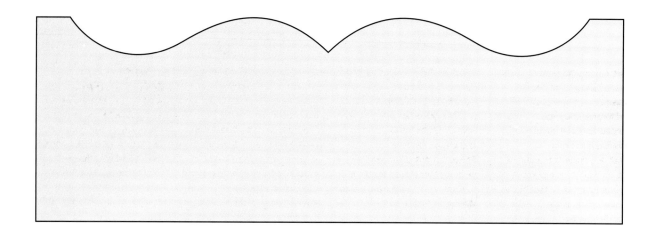

p116 Planter covers

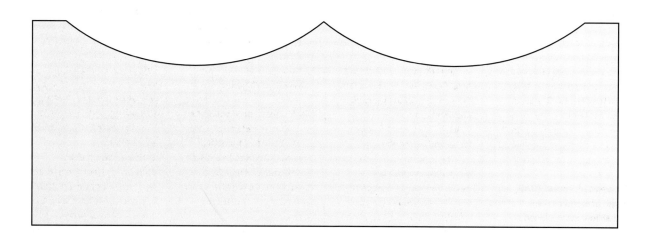

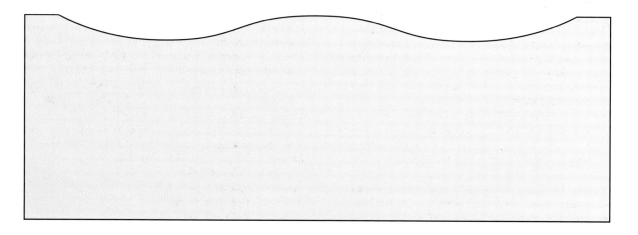

Glossary

Arris A sharp edge where two surfaces meet at an angle.

Batten A strip of wood, often used to describe wood attached to a wall for holding a component in place.

Bevel Any angle, other than a right angle, cut on a piece of wood or found on a tool blade; to cut such an angle.

Chamfer A small 45-degree bevel planed along the edge of a piece of wood to make it less sharp; to plane such a bevel.

Check A split in the surface of wood that is the result of unequal drying.

Counterbore A hole drilled into wood to allow the entire head of a screw or bolt to end up below the surface; to drill such a hole.

Cross grain Grain that does not follow the main grain direction in a workpiece.

Cup On a piece of wood, to bend, usually across the width, as a direct result of shrinkage.

Dowel A short, round length of wood that is fitted into holes in two pieces of wood to hold them together; to fit such a piece of wood.

Doweling A long length of wood for doweling, often used for decoration, in plate racks, shelves, etc.

Dressed all round (DAR) A length of wood or plank that has had all four sides planed before being sold—the dimensions given, however, are for the wood before it was planed, so DAR length is smaller.

Dressed two sides (D2S) A length of wood or plank that has had two opposing sides planed before being sold.

Dry assembling Fitting together or assembling workpieces without fixing or gluing them, to check for an accurate fit and that all angles are true before final fixing.

End grain The irregular surface of wood that is exposed after cutting across the fibers.

Face edge The surface planed square to the face side.

Face side On a piece of wood, the flat surface (usually planed) from which all measurements and angles are taken.

Fence A device attached to a workpiece or tool to enable a straight line to be cut parallel to the edge of the wood— proprietary fences are available for many power tools, but they can be homemade.

Galvanized Screws or nails covered with a protective layer of zinc, used to prevent rusting in outdoor projects.

Grain The direction or alignment of the fibers in a piece of wood.

Groove A narrow channel cut along a piece of wood in the direction of the grain; to cut such a channel.

Hardboard A slightly flexible man-made board, mostly used for the back panels of shelves, cabinets, etc.

Hardwood Wood that comes from deciduous, broad-leafed trees—not necessarily harder than softwood.

Hone To sharpen the edge of a blade and create the final cutting edge on it.

Jig A device, often home-made, for holding a piece of work in position and enabling repeated working to be done.

Kerf The cut made in wood by a saw.

Knock-down (KD) fitting A metal or plastic fitting for joining two pieces of wood at right angles. KD fittings are designed to be easily taken apart, and are mostly used in flat-pack and kitchen furniture.

Laminate A flat surface made by bonding different layers together, such as plastic, melamine, etc.; to make such a board.

Marine plywood or board A plywood made with water-resistant hardwood layers and strong glue, used for exterior projects and those where moisture and condensation may occur.

Medium-density fiberboard (MDF) A versatile, smooth-surfaced man-made board, produced by binding wood dust together with glue.

Miter A corner joint for which two pieces of wood are cut with bevels of equal angles, usually 45 degrees; to cut such a joint.

Molding A length of wood, either hardwood or softwood, that has a shaped profile.

Offcut A piece of scrap wood left over after a workpiece has been cut or shaped.

Pare To remove fine shavings from a piece of wood by hand-manipulation of a chisel.

Particleboard A coarse-finished man-made board, often faced with melamine laminate or hardwood veneer and used in inexpensive furniture and kitchen units.

Patina The subtle color and texture acquired by lumber as it ages.

Pilot hole A small hole drilled into wood that acts as a guide for the thread of a woodscrew.

Plywood A strong man-made board produced by gluing thin layers of board together—often faced with hardwood or softwood veneer.

Primer The first coat of paint on bare wood, designed to seal the surface and provide a base for subsequent coats.

Rabbet A recess, step or groove, usually rectangular, that is cut into a piece of wood to allow a mating piece to be inserted there.

Size A weak solution of glue—in woodworking, used mainly in applying metal leaf or similar.

Skew Describes a nail or screw that is driven in to one or more pieces of wood at an angle other than a right angle; to drive in a nail or screw in this way, usually intentionally.

Slat A narrow, usually thin, length of wood used as part of an identical series to form a fence, chair seat, and back, etc.

Softwood Wood that comes from coniferous trees—this is not necessarily softer than hardwood.

Splitting out The result of a cutter or bit cutting through the other side opposite the face side.

Stile The vertical side pieces of a door or window frame.

Stock The main body or handle of a tool, usually made of hardwood or plastic.

Tang The sharp, pointed end of a chisel or rasp that is driven into the stock or handle.

Template A pattern or shape, usually drawn on card, paper, or thin board, used as a guide for accurate marking on wood or man-made boards, especially when more than one identical piece is required.

Tongue-and-groove A joint in which a thin tongue of wood on one piece of wood is fitted into a matching groove on another —mainly used in doors and wall panels.

True Describes when something is exact, e.g. a true right angle is perfectly accurate; to smooth perfectly flat with a plane, chisel, or sander.

Wallboard A man-made board where two layers of thick paper or card sandwich a layer of plaster—wallboard is primarily used to make cavity walls.

Winding Describes a warped or twisted length of wood.

With the grain Working wood along the direction or alignment of the fibers.

Workpiece A piece of wood or project that is unfinished and still being worked on.